marvelous
mosaics
for home &
garden

George W. Shannon &
Pat Torlen

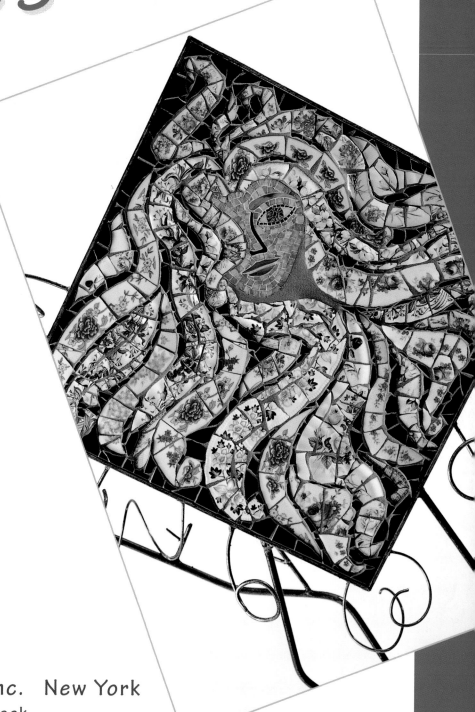

Sterling Publishing Co., Inc.   New York
A Sterling/Tamos Book

A Sterling/Tamos Book

First paperback edition published in 2001 by
Sterling Publishing Company, Inc.
387 Park Avenue South, New York, N.Y. 10016

TAMOS Books Inc.
300 Wales Avenue,Winnipeg, MB Canada R2M 2S9

10 9 8 7 6 5 4 3

Originally released in hard cover under the title
Marvelous Mosaics with Unusual Materials
© 2000 by George W. Shannon & Pat Torlen
Distributed in Canada by Sterling Publishing
c/o Canadian Manda Group, One Atlantic Avenue,
Suite 105, Toronto, Ontario, Canada, M6K 3E7
Distributed in Great Britain by Chrysalis Books
64 Brewery Road, London N7 9NT, England
Distributed in Australia by Capricorn Link (Australia)
Pty Ltd.
P.O. Box 704, Windsor, NSW 2756 Australia

Design A. O. Osen
Photography Jerry Grajewski, Steve Daniels,
grajewski.fotograph

Tamos Books Inc. acknowledges the financial support of
the Government of Canada through the Book Publishing
Industry Development Program for our publishing
activities.

Printed in China

ISBN 1-895569-72-9

Dedication
for Brianna Stark

Acknowledgments
Special thanks to Len Dushnicky, Susan
Green, Wendy Meyer, Jayne Nixon, Betty
Shannon, Lynn Sinclair, Brianna Stark, and
Herbert Strasser for their creative input and
assistance in constructing the projects; Pete
and Helen Peters of Classic Fireplaces,
Winnipeg, Canada for supplying the electric
fireplace, mantle, and support structure.

All projects in this book are original designs
by On The Edge Glass Studio.

The advice and directions given in this book
have been carefully checked, prior to printing,
by the Author as well as the Publisher.
Nevertheless, no guarantee can be given as
to project outcome due to the possible
differences in materials and the Author and
Publisher will not be responsible for the
results.

If you prefer to work in metric measurements,
to convert inches to millimeters multiply by
25.4.

Contents

Introduction

Mosaic art has adorned churches and cathedrals, private dwellings, and public spaces for several thousand years. Design styles, materials, tools, and techniques have changed and evolved through the centuries, but what is constant about this art is that images are brought to life by the play of light over the mosaic surface. Individual mosaic pieces are arranged so that light is reflected, transmitted, and transformed when it strikes the various textures and colors and the viewer appreciates the whole effect.

Traditionally, mosaics were fabricated by skilled craftsmen adhering small cubes of glass, marble, ceramic or stone tiles, pebbles, and semi-precious stones to a larger, relatively smooth surface. Roman and Hellenistic Greek mosaic artists were among the first to assemble individual units of material, referred to as tesserae, into a variety of complex and intricate patterns and motifs creating floor installations and wall murals depicting acts of heroism, myths, and interpretations of paintings. These artists developed and refined many of the techniques still in use today while creating remarkable feats of tonal shading in mosaic installations comprised primarily of marble, limestone, and other stone materials.

In the fourth and fifth centuries A.D. early Christian wall mosaics utilized glass tesserae which provided a greater range and color intensity than in the earlier marble mosaics. Decorated fountains, altars, and grand scale wall murals were now possible with the evolution of mosaic art. The use of gold and silver smalti, made by sandwiching thin pieces of the precious metals between the glass, added another dimension to the art form. Byzantine mosaic art contributed the use of gold and silver cubes, tilted to illuminate and reflect light in special ways to add a new perspective and dimension to mosaic artwork. Some of the greatest expressions of mosaic art occurred during this era. But with the decline of the Byzantine civilization, production of these grand mosaics was greatly reduced and less expensive painted wall murals began to take their place.

By the eighteenth century interest in mosaic art was again apparent and Rome became a center for mosaic revival as preserved in works created for St. Peter's Basilica and miniature mosaics comprised of minute tesserae. The arrival of the Art Nouveau period during the 1890s and the early 1900s brought further changes to mosaic style. Artists began creating works reminiscent of the organic curves and shapes found in nature as well as bold geometric lines and configurations. This led to a more informal and spontaneous composition style not previously demonstrated.

Modern mosaic artists have readily adopted all these techniques, but they seek to use them in different ways and push the art form in new directions. Their vision is multifaceted, creating fine mosaic artworks as well as decorating and beautifying utilitarian objects. The projects in this book explore diverse and challenging mosaic techniques as well as extend traditional methods into different parameters. Traditional mosaic and ceramic tiles are still used to make beautiful art pieces but with the addition of different materials such as broken china, art glass, glass nuggets and jewels, mirror, stones, fossils, shells, and other found objects. Today the mosaic artist has the freedom to make items that are new and original as a means of personal expression and accomplishment. A fresh perspective is achieved with translucent mosaic window hanging projects that allow light to shine through the mosaic instead of being reflected off the surface. This technique is a contemporary approach to mosaic construction and gives depth and interest to window hangings, lamp shades, and other decorative objects.

As well as utilizing a wide range of materials the twenty projects in this book demonstrate several methods of construction. The finished pieces are all individual creations and they can be constructed from the patterns given or used to inspire future designs by the maker. Complete instructions of all techniques are included and step-by-step directions show the crafter every aspect of mosaic making for these unique, beautiful mosaics for the home and garden. The popularity of mosaic art is currently in a period of revival and transformation, and artists, craftsmen, and hobbyists are exploring the unlimited possibilities for the creative and functional expression that mosaic construction offers.

Mosaic Construction

Sourcing the items required for constructing mosaics is easy. Useful materials and tools are commonly found around the home and at local hardware stores or home and garden centers. Many retail outlets that cater to stained glass craftsmen and hobbyists have knowledgeable staff to give expert advice for proper tool selection and materials needed. Check your telephone directory yellow pages for the nearest stores and for those establishments offering mail order service. Secondhand stores and garage sales can also be a source for inexpensive materials that are unique and unusual and other craftsmen can often supply source information as well.

Materials

Vitreous glass mosaic tiles   These ¾ in square tesserae have a flat top surface with beveled edges and slight underside grooves to aid adhesion and are available in a wide selection of opaque colors including rich translucent shades with swirls of sparkling copper. The tiles are durable in most climate conditions and are suitable for most projects either indoors or outside.

Glass   Some mosaic projects in this book utilize art glass and mirrored glass instead of traditional tesserae materials. Simple cutting techniques make it easy to cut and shape, and art glass comes in an endless variety of color combinations.

Glass nuggets, marbles, and jewels   These glass accent pieces come in a wide selection of colors, sizes, and shapes.

Ceramic tiles and chinaware   Many types of commercial ceramic mosaic tiles are readily available, usually on sheets with a paper or net backing. Tile size ranges from ¼ in to 4 in squares and can be used in sheet form to cover large areas quickly or removed from the backing and used individually. Specialty ceramic tiles or pieces of household china and crockery add special interest to mosaic projects.

Stone   Pieces of marble, slate, granite, and other stone materials as well as pebbles and small rocks can be used to accent mosaic pieces.

Found objects   Collect bits of beach glass, shells, fossils, photos, jewelry pieces, and other mementos to personalize a mosaic project.

Adhesives   There are many types of adhesive and glue for bonding mosaic pieces to the base/support structure. Read the labels and choose the adhesive suitable for the project, keeping in mind the type of base material used and the location and purpose of the finished mosaic. Use a non-toxic adhesive whenever possible.

Mastics (used for many projects in this book) are premixed glues for adhering tiles to interior walls.

Thin-set mortars are comprised of portland cement, sand, and water. Latex polymer additive can be used in place of, or in combination with, the water for greater strength, flexibility, and water and impact resistance. Thin-set mortars

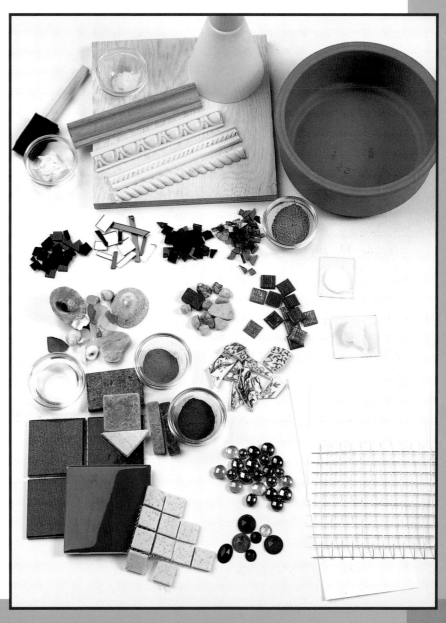

are essential for floors and outdoor installations.

Clear silicone adhesive is used for the translucent mosaic projects in this book. When applied correctly this glue is not visible on projects.

All-purpose white glue and carpenter's glue are non-toxic and are suitable for small indoor projects including wall hangings, plaques, and trivets.

Grout Grout is used to fill the spaces (interstices) between individual mosaic pieces. It provides additional strength, covers sharp edges on the tesserae, helps to level the surface of the mosaic, and gives a finished look. Grout comes in many colors or add tint for the desired shade.

Pre-mixed mortar cement Pre-mixed cement, found at hardware stores and home and garden centers, is used to make the mosaic garden stone projects in this book. This is a mixture of portland cement, sand, and water (and/or latex polymer additive) that is used to give the top surface of a garden stone a smooth, even finish. Use additional portland cement for more strength and durability.

Tints Add tint powders to grout and cement to produce colors not readily available. Colored latex and acrylic paints can also be used to tint cement.

Sealants Sealants protect grout and mosaic surfaces from moisture damage and scuff marks. Porous materials such as unglazed ceramic tile, terra-cotta, marble, slate, and limestone should be sealed before grouting to avoid staining. Many interior projects including wall hangings and translucent mosaics will not require a sealant. Re-application of sealant may be required periodically to compensate for climate conditions and day-to-day wear.

Petroleum jelly A thin layer of petroleum jelly rubbed onto the sides and bottom of a garden stone mold will ease stone removal.

Clear adhesive-backed vinyl After laying the mosaic pattern on the work surface, adhesive-backed vinyl (sandblasting resist or contact paper) is cut to the size and shape of the mosaic, the wax paper backing is removed, and the vinyl is placed over the pattern with the adhesive back facing upward. The pattern can still be seen as the tesserae are laid onto the adhesive backing in the appropriate position. This prevents movement of the pieces when cement is poured.

Reinforcement wire For additional strength and durability, place a piece of galvanized hardware cloth into the form when pouring the cement. Use mesh sizes from $\frac{1}{2}$ in to 1 in.

Plywood and wood moldings Molds or frames for some project construction require $\frac{1}{2}$ in to $\frac{3}{4}$ in exterior grade plywood or other wood moldings and trims.

Bases/support structures Mosaics can be built upon wood furniture, pre-cut mirrors, concrete pedestals and birdbaths, glass and china vessels, terra-cotta pots, picture frames, and many other items. Floor installations require cement backerboard as the foundation for laying tiles and mosaics. Suggestions and ideas for bases are given with each project and instructions are supplied for support structure construction.

Equipment

Permanent waterproof fine-tipped marker This tool is used for outlining pattern pieces on glass. Use a silver or gold marker for dark and opaque glass.

China marker Use this marker to indicate where ceramic tiles and other porous mosaic materials need to be shaped and trimmed.

Drawing equipment Use a small square, pencil, eraser, cork-backed ruler or straightedge, tracing paper, carbon paper, marking pen, compass, scissors, and light cardstock for making pattern copies, drawing and scoring straight lines, verifying angles and proper alignment, and making templates.

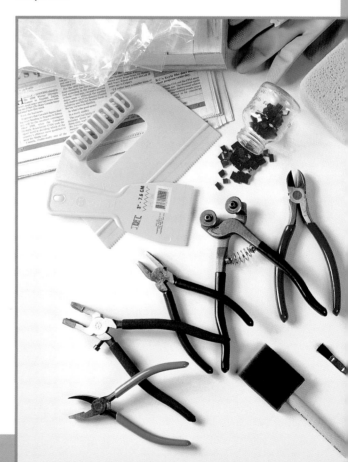

Traditional glass cutter   This is required to accurately score and break individual pieces of glass to fit project patterns. The two most common types are dry-wheel and oil-fed. An inexpensive steel wheel cutter has a larger steel cutting wheel and is usually disposed of after each project. A lubricant must be applied to the steel wheel before each score is made. Self-lubricating cutters have smaller cutting wheels made of carbide steel and a reservoir for oil, are more expensive, but last for many years. The smaller size wheel can better follow the contours and uneven surfaces of art glass. Popular models have either a traditional pencil-shaped barrel or a pistol grip handle.

Glass mosaic cutters (nippers)   This plier-shaped cutter has two long-lasting and replaceable carbide wheel jaws and is used scissor-like to cut and shape glass tesserae.

Breaking/grozing pliers   Breaking pliers have flat smooth jaws for gripping and breaking off scored pieces of glass and thin ceramic tiles. Grozing pliers have narrow, flat, serrated jaws to nibble unwanted bits along the edge of the glass. Combination pliers combine the uses of breaking and grozing pliers. The top jaw is flat and the bottom jaw is concave—both are serrated.

Running pliers   These pliers apply equal pressure on both sides of a long and straight or gently curved score line forcing the score to "run" or break along its length. With practice, they can be used to start breaks on more difficult score lines. Metal running pliers have a concave jaw (placed on the top side of glass) and a convex jaw (placed on underside of glass) that allows the breaking of narrow pieces of glass. They also have the strength to carry a run over a longer distance. Some pliers have a central guide mark on the top jaw to assist in aligning the pliers on top of the glass correctly or draw a guide mark with a permanent waterproof marking pen.

Tile cutters

Tile nippers are similar to glass mosaic cutters and can nip out small curves and shapes.

Snap cutters are used to score straight cuts and snap the tile into two pieces.

Mini-cutters resemble pliers but have a steel cutting wheel for scoring and jaws for snapping small tiles into smaller pieces.

Water-cooled wet saws cut tiles and stone quickly and accurately. They can be purchased or rented.

Carborundum stone   This small rectangular block composed of hard carbon compound and silicon is used to file sharp edges off tesserae. It must be kept wet to prevent minute particles from becoming airborne.

Diamond pads   These foam pads are impregnated with diamond particles and are used to remove sharp edges from tesserae. They must be kept wet to prevent minute particles from becoming airborne.

Wet/dry sandpaper   This sandpaper is coated with silicon carbide. Moistened with water, it can be used to take the sharpness off cut tesserae edges.

Glass grinder and band saw   Complex and detailed glass shapes are now possible with the aid of a glass grinder with diamond-coated bit or a band saw with a diamond-coated blade. Both machines have a water reservoir to trap the dust produced and prevent hazardous glass particles from becoming airborne.

NOTE A glass grinder or band saw is not essential to complete the glass mosaic projects in this book although these tools can be used. A carborundum stone or wet/dry sandpaper is sufficient to smooth mosaic materials, or make a slight design change to simplify cutting a pattern piece.

Small containers or jars   These can be used to keep tesserae pieces sorted by color and size.

Molds and forms   Many commercial molds and forms are available on the market for the construction of mosaics or

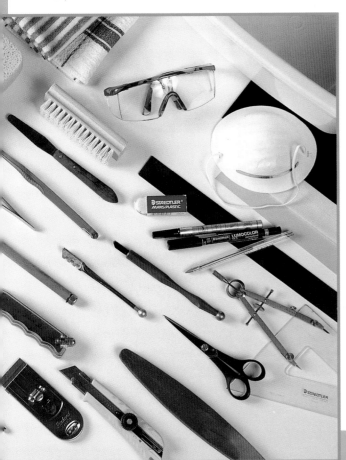

make your own, following instructions included in this book. Inexpensive alternatives include plastic food storage

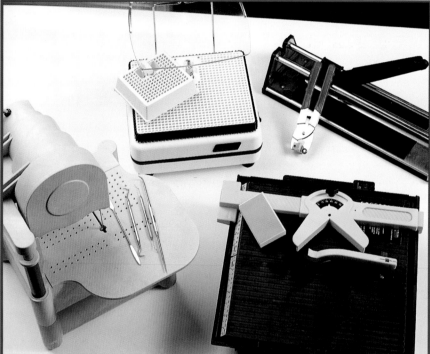

containers and springform baking pans for garden stone forms.

Mixing containers and manual mixers   There are a number of inexpensive manual cement mixers available for making small batches of cement that may be purchased at garden centers or craft stores.

Tweezers and dental tools   These instruments are useful for positioning small pieces of tesserae on patterns and clear adhesive-backed vinyl. Also use dental tools for cleaning adhesives, cements, and grouts from small crevices and hard-to-reach corners.

Wire cutters (snips or sidecutters)   This tool cuts reinforcement wire for mosaic garden stones.

Trowels and palette knives   These tools help to apply and evenly spread adhesive. Apply adhesives to the base/support structure with the flat edge of a trowel and then make ridges with the notched side. Palette knives and smaller margin trowels are used for buttering the back of tesserae, applying adhesive to hard-to-reach areas, and smoothing grout joints.

Sponges   To prepare for grouting, wipe a water-moistened sponge across the surface of the mosaic. After grouting, a

damp sponge wipes excess grout off mosaic surfaces before the grout is allowed to dry.

Brushes   Toothbrushes and small craft and scrub brushes can be used to apply adhesive or clean and polish the project.

Utility knife   This knife can be used to trim clear adhesive-backed vinyl, cut out paper pattern pieces, or clear away excessive adhesive and grout.

Razor blades/paint scrapers   Use these tools to scrape away excess adhesive, grout, and cement from the surface of mosaic projects.

Polishing cloths   Clean and dry lint-free cotton cloths are used to buff the finished mosaic surface.

Newspaper   Rubbing the surface of a finished mosaic garden stone with newspaper lifts and removes debris while polishing at the same time. Do not use for cleaning light-colored grouts.

Woodworking tools   Some woodworking tools are required if you wish to make your own molds or base/support structures. See the instructions provided in this book.

The Work Area

Choose a comfortable space equipped with a large, sturdy table or workbench with a smooth, level work surface (preferably plywood) adjusted to working height (around waist level) with good overhead lighting (natural light, if possible). Area should have an electrical outlet with grounded circuit for glass grinder and wet saw, an easy-to-clean hard surfaced floor, and a rack or wooden bin with dividers to store sheets of glass in an upright position. Store smaller pieces in a cardboard box.

Good ventilation (window/fan) is required when working with adhesives, grouts, and cements, and access to water is needed for mixing grouts and cements, using grinding or cutting equipment, and cleaning projects.

Have a supply of newspaper to cover work surface for easy cleaning and a bench brush and dust pan to clear work surface of glass chips and other debris.

NOTE   Try to mix concrete outdoors whenever possible to prevent the active ingredients and dust in the cement mixture from entering your work area and/or home.

Safety Practices and Equipment

To work safely while building a mosaic check these simple rules.

1   Always wear safety glasses or goggles when cutting glass and tesserae.

2   Wear a full-length work apron at every stage in the mosaic construction process.

3   Wear closed shoes to protect feet.

4   Pre-mixed mortar cement compounds form a caustic, calcium hydroxide solution when mixed with water. When handling cement powders and wet mixtures, avoid contact with skin or eyes by wearing tight-fitting safety glasses or goggles, rubber or latex gloves, and protective clothing (long-sleeved work shirts and full-length pants are recommended).

5   Use soap and water to wash any skin area and clothing that comes in contact with wet cement mixtures or concrete. Wash work clothes and aprons separately from other clothing.

6   Wear a dust mask or respirator when handling or mixing cement and grout powders. For pertinent information on respirators and filters, visit a local safety supply store.

7   Work outdoors or in a well-ventilated area when mixing cement or working with adhesives. Whenever possible use materials that are non-toxic.

8   To avoid the possibility of ingesting cement and grout dusts and powders, do not eat, drink, or smoke while working with these agents. Keep hands away from mouth and face. Wash exposed skin areas with soap and water after each work session.

9   Cover all cuts and scrapes with an adhesive plaster when working with cement or grout to prevent skin irritation.

10   Clean the work area and floor surface with a damp mop or wet sponge to prevent cement and grout powders and dusts from becoming airborne.

11   Carry large glass pieces in a vertical position with one hand supporting the sheet from below and the other hand steadying the sheet from the side. Wear protective gloves when moving larger sheets.

12   Wear hearing protection when using loud machinery such as a wet saw.

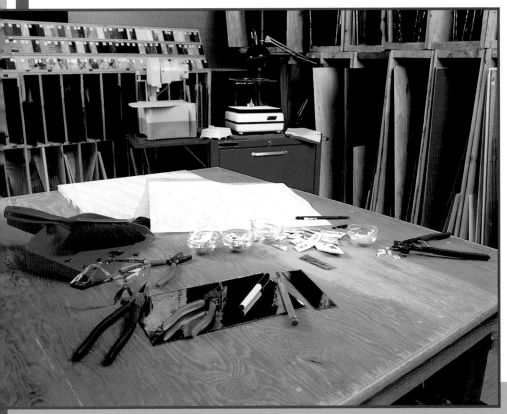

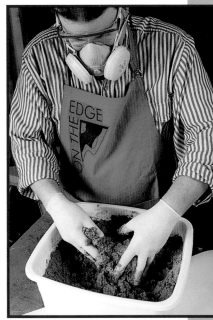

Basic Techniques

Making copies of patterns

Prepare two or three copies of each pattern chosen. Verify each copy with the original pattern for accuracy.

Photocopying Digital photocopiers make true copies of the original. Many photocopiers can also enlarge or reduce patterns.

Tracing Lay tracing vellum over the pattern and trace the lines of the design. Use carbon sheets to make multiple copies. Lay a sheet of paper on the work surface and place a carbon face down overtop. For each copy required, add another layer of paper and carbon. Place the project pattern on top and fasten in place, using push pins or tape. Press firmly to transfer image through each layer of paper.

Blueprinting Trace the pattern onto drawing vellum and take it to a blueprinting firm to make exact copies. Verify that a pattern requiring mosaic pieces of a specific size and/or shape fits the copied pattern before beginning the project.

Overhead and opaque projectors Projectors can distort patterns. Use this method as a guideline only.

NOTE Protect pattern copies by having them laminated. Keep smaller patterns dry during the grinding stage by placing them inside vinyl sheet protectors or covering them with a clear adhesive-backed vinyl.

Selecting mosaic materials for a project

Various combinations of design, color, texture, and light determine the look of a finished mosaic piece. Here are a few helpful guidelines.

1 View mosaic materials in lighting conditions similar to those where the finished project will be displayed. Choose most materials for their reflective surface qualities except translucent glass mosaics that use art glass that transmits light and color.

2 Choose opaque materials or textured art glasses that will obscure the adhesives and cements (these will show through translucent mosaics) used to adhere the tesserae to the base/support structure of the mosaic. If a translucent glass is chosen consider one with an iridescent finish that reflects light and camouflages the adhesive beneath it.

3 Vibrant and colorful materials make a mosaic piece come alive. The larger the project, the greater the

number of color variations, textures, and materials that can be introduced. In smaller projects, focus on two or three selections. View the materials side by side to see how the colors and textures affect each other. Take into consideration the color of grout or cement used for the project.

4 For garden stone projects, use mosaic materials with one smooth surface. Pieces that are heavily textured will not stick as readily to the adhesive-backed vinyl and may become partially or completely buried in the cement.

NOTE Material quantities listed for individual projects are a close approximation for each pattern. Having additional materials on hand will allow for matching patterns, grains, and textures or for possible breakage.

Transferring pattern shapes onto glass

Draw the outline of the piece to be cut directly onto the glass with a permanent waterproof fine-tipped marker. Position the pattern piece to avoid waste but take into account the grain or texture and how it will flow with the other pieces around it. Leave approximately ¼ in around the piece so the breaking pliers will have material to grasp when breaking the score line.

For many translucent and light-colored opalescent glasses transfer the pattern by placing the glass sheet directly on the pattern copy and tracing the design lines with the marker. A light box can help illuminate the pattern from below.

For opaque glass the pattern can be transferred onto the glass using one of three methods.

1 Using scissors or utility knife, cut the pattern piece from an extra copy of the project pattern. Place pattern piece on glass and trace around the outside edges with the marker.

2 Make a template of the pieces to be cut (using tracing method described above) and use marker to trace around template perimeter onto the glass. Use cardstock, lightweight cardboard, or 2mm or 3mm float glass (windowpane) for making the template.

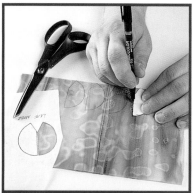

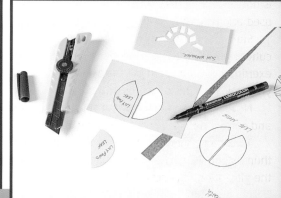

NOTE   When cutting out a piece from the pattern copy or making a template, cut on the *inside* of the pattern lines.

3   Place a carbon sheet face down on the glass with the pattern on top. Go over pattern lines with a pen or pencil to transfer pattern outline onto the glass. Go over the carbon lines with the marker.

NOTE

• Dressmaker's carbon tracing paper comes in several colors. Use a light color (yellow) for tracing pattern shapes onto dark glass to make lines more visible for cutting.

• Permanent markers may be difficult to see on dark glass. Use silver or gold paint marker for better visibility.

Cutting and shaping glass

Cutting glass using a glass cutter   Cutting a piece of glass involves scoring and breaking. Score the outline by running the wheel of a glass cutter along the traced line. Apply even pressure on either side of the score line to break piece away.

Cutting glass properly is a skill that can be attained with a little effort. Draw cutting patterns A, B, C, and D (pp12, 13) on a 12 in by 12 in sheet of 3mm float glass (windowpane glass). Practice scoring and breaking techniques using this exercise to gauge cutting flow and amount of pressure to exert.

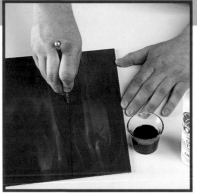

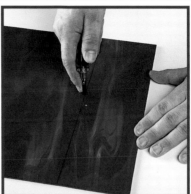

Pencil style cutter, oil-fed, and held as a pencil.

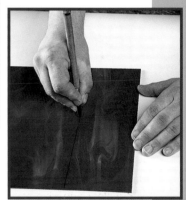

Disposable cutter rests between the index and middle fingers with the ball of the thumb placed to push cutter along. Apply lubricant to the cutter head before each score.

Pistol grip cutter held in palm of hand with the thumb resting on top of the barrel and index finger guiding cutter head.

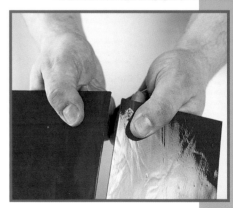

Basic rules of glass cutting

1   Wear safety glasses and a work apron. Stand in an upright position in front of the worktable.

2   Work on a clean, level, non-skid work surface covered with newspaper.

3   Always place the glass smooth side up, on which the pattern has been traced with the marker. Make sure the surface of the glass is clean and free of any debris.

4   Hold the cutter in your writing hand perpendicular to the glass, not tilted to the left or right. Run the cutter away from your body and inside the pattern lines, applying steady pressure as you score. The pressure should be coming mainly from your shoulder, not the hand. Lubricate the wheel of the cutter before each score if it is not self-oiling. How you hold the cutter in your hand will depend on what type is used and what grip is the most comfortable.

5   Start and finish the score line at an edge of the glass. Do not stop or lift your cutter from the glass surface before the score is completed. Use a fluid motion, exerting constant, even pressure. Because of their shape, some pieces will require that you make a series of scores and breaks.

6   Never go over a score line a second time. To do so will damage the cutter wheel and compromise the score line, increasing the likelihood of an unsuccessful break.

7   To complete the break, grasp the glass with a hand on each side of the score line, thumbs parallel to the score, knuckles touching. Roll wrists up and outward, breaking the glass along the scored line.

Holding glass, as shown, break glass along the scored line.

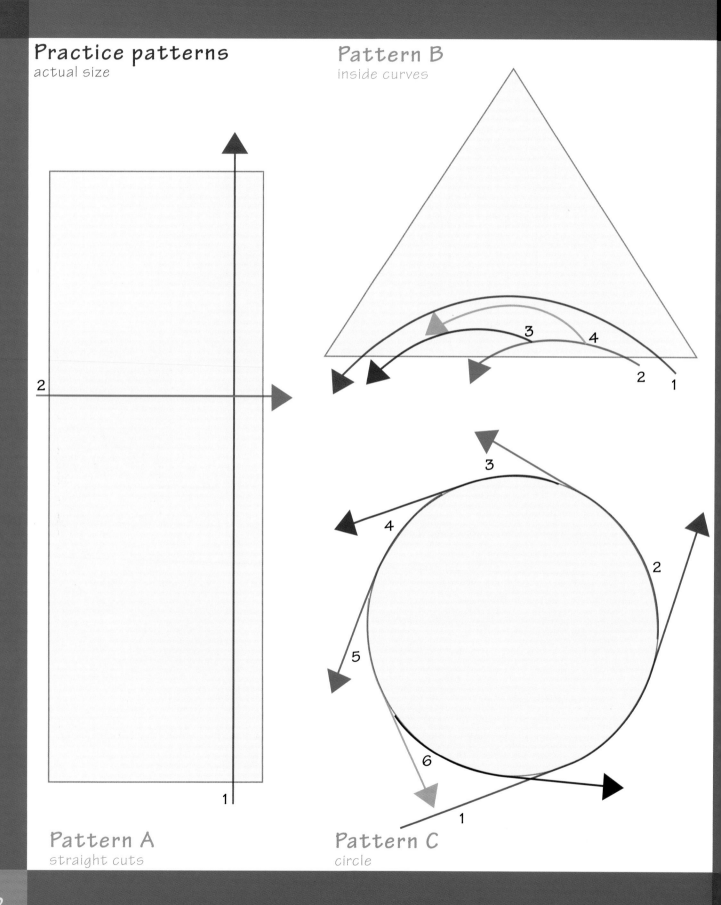

Practice patterns
actual size

Pattern B
inside curves

Pattern A
straight cuts

Pattern C
circle

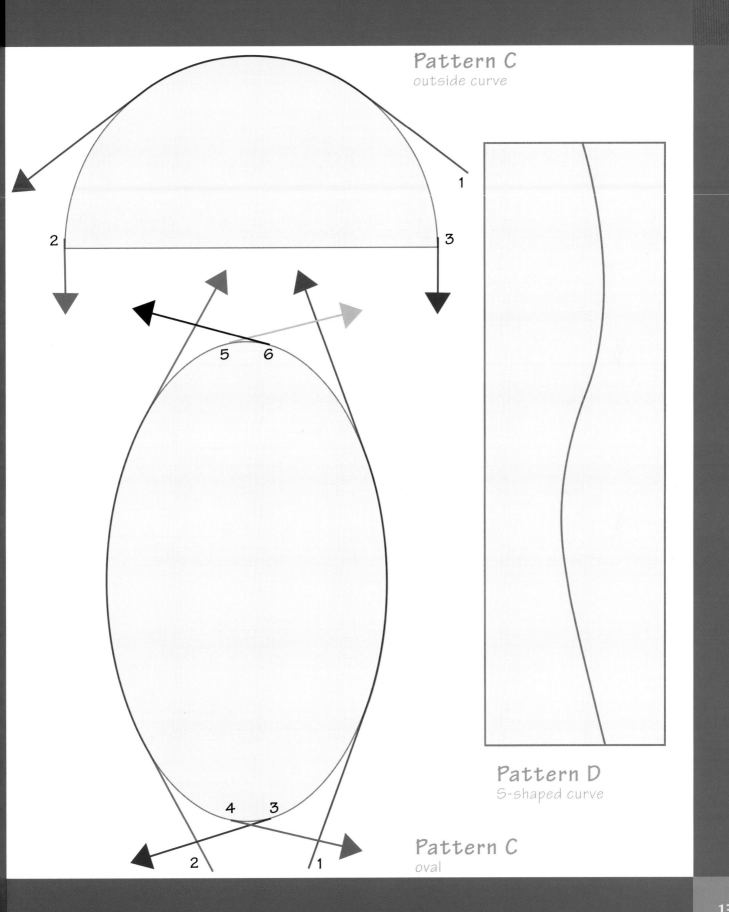

Pattern C
outside curve

Pattern D
S-shaped curve

Pattern C
oval

Breaking glass on a score line

Using running pliers   Many square and rectangular pieces are required for some projects in this book. Use running pliers to break straight lines and slight curves or start a break at either end of a score line. Metal running pliers are preferable. The slightly concave jaw must be placed on the topside of the glass and the convex jaw on the underside.

1   Position running pliers so score line is centered and glass is approximately $\frac{1}{2}$ in to $\frac{3}{4}$ in inside the jaws.

2   Gently squeeze handles and score will run (travel), breaking glass into two pieces. If the run does not go the full length of the score line, repeat the procedure at the other end of the score line. The two runs should meet, causing the score line to break completely.

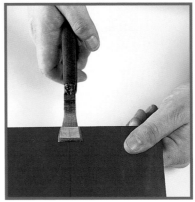 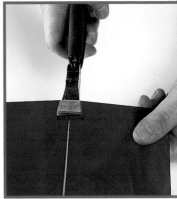

For breaking straight lines or slight curves on glass, use the running pliers.

Using breaking pliers or combination pliers   Breaking pliers have two identical flat, smooth jaws that can be placed on either side of the glass. Combination pliers have a flat top jaw and a curved bottom jaw—both jaws are serrated.

1   Position the pliers perpendicular to the score line and as close as possible without touching it. Start at either end of the score line (not the middle).

2   Use an out-and-downward pulling motion on the pliers to break the glass.

3   When using two sets of pliers to break apart two smaller pieces of glass, place the pliers on the glass on either side of the score line and opposite to each other. Hold one set of pliers steady and use an out-and-downward pulling motion with the other set to separate the glass piece.

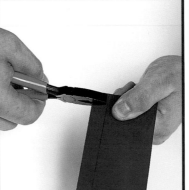 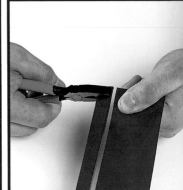

Combination pliers or breaking pliers are positioned perpendicular to the score line.

Breaking a score line by tapping underneath   Sometimes long and/or curving score lines refuse to break. Tapping may cause small chips and fractures along the score line and, if not done carefully, may result in the score running in a different direction. Use the following method as a last resort.

1   Hold the glass close to the surface of the worktable. Using the ball at the end of the cutter, gently strike the glass from the underside, directly underneath the score line. Once the score begins to run, continue tapping ahead of the run until it reaches the other end of the score line.

2   Using hands or a pair of pliers, separate the scored piece from the main sheet of glass.

Scoring a straight line   To score straight lines, use a cork-backed metal ruler with a thick, rounded edge as a

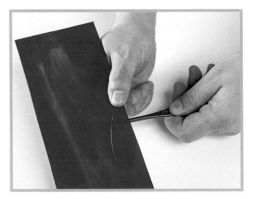

As a last resort, difficult to break glass may be tapped underneath the score line to urge the run to begin.

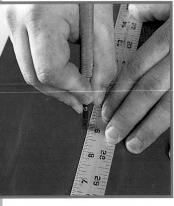

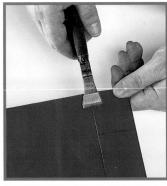

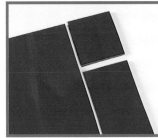

Place the straightedge parallel with the line to be scored. Cutting squares and rectangles requires several straight cuts.

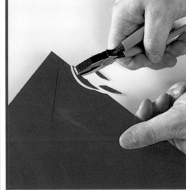

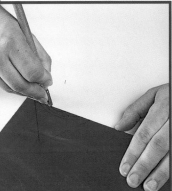

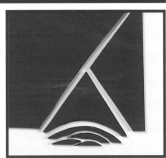

Cutting inside curves requires a series of concave cuts. Attempt the most difficult cut before breaking the piece away from the main sheet of glass.

straightedge.

1 Mark the line to be cut and position straightedge parallel and approximately ⅛ in from the line (exact distance is determined by width of the cutter head).

2 Align the head of the glass cutter with the straightedge, positioning wheel on the marked line.

3 Holding straightedge firmly on the surface of the glass, make the score line by either pulling the cutter toward the body or by pushing it away. Maintain even pressure.

4 Break the score line, using one of the methods from p14.

Cutting squares and rectangles   Glass is difficult to cut at a 90 degree angle. Use a series of straight scores and breaks to cut square and rectangular pieces.

1 Trace pattern A (p12) onto the glass, aligning one of the sides of the pattern with the edge of the glass.

2 Score along the other side of the pattern piece and proceed to break the score line (p14).

3 Score and break any remaining cut required to achieve the shape of the pattern piece.

Cutting inside curves   Attempt these most difficult cuts first, before cutting the piece away from the main sheet of glass.

1 Trace pattern piece B (p12) onto the glass. Position the outer edges of the curve so they align with the edge of the glass.

2 Score the inside curve of the pattern piece but do not break it out.

3 Make several smaller concave score lines (scallops) between the initial score line and the outside edge of the glass.

4 Using breaker or combination pliers, start removing the scallops, one at a time, beginning with the one closest to the edge of the glass. Use a pulling action with the pliers rather than a downward motion. Remember to position the jaws of the pliers at either end of the score line and not in the middle.

5 Continue to break away the scallops until the initial score line is reached. Remove it and proceed to score and break away the pattern piece from the larger glass sheet.

NOTE   Use tapping method (p14) to run a score line to break out stubborn pieces.

Cutting circles, ovals, and outside curves

1 Trace pattern C (pp12, 13) onto the glass, leaving ½ in from the outside edge of the glass.

2 Make an initial score line to separate the pattern piece from the sheet of glass. The score line will go from the

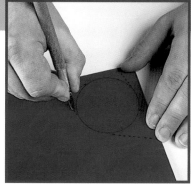

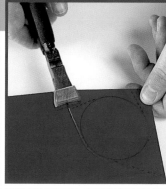

outside edge of the glass to the circle and follow its perimeter a short distance and then head off on a tangent to an opposing edge of the glass (*see* line 1). Break away this piece.

3 The second score line will follow around the circle for a short distance (approximately one-sixth of the perimeter) and then leave on a tangent to the outside edge (*see* line 2).

4 Repeat step 3, scoring and breaking the glass in a pinwheel fashion, until the circle shape has been formed (*see* lines 3, 4, 5, and 6).

5 Small jagged edges where a score line was started or ended can be ground off with a glass grinder, nibbled away with combination pliers (*see* Grozing, p19), or filed off with a carborundum stone.

6 This method for cutting circular pieces can be adapted to cut outside curves and ovals.

Scoring and breaking S-shaped curves

1 Trace pattern D (p13) onto the glass, placing one of the sides against the edge of the glass.

2 Score the S-shape cut first.

3 Align running pliers with the score line. Squeeze only hard enough to start the run. Repeat the procedure at the opposite end of the score line. If both runs meet, separate the resulting two pieces by hand. If runs do not meet, gently tap along score line on underside of the glass.

4 Score and break out remaining cuts.

Using glass mosaic cutters (nippers)

These are used to cut and shape many of the smaller pieces in a mosaic project.

1 Use a glass cutter and breaking or running pliers to cut a strip or smaller piece of glass away from a larger sheet. The cut-away piece must be slightly larger than the pattern piece that you require.

2 With a permanent waterproof fine-tipped marker, trace the outline of the pattern piece onto the glass.

3 Grip the mosaic cutters in your writing hand and hold the glass in the opposite hand. Using a scissor-like motion, nip away portions of glass along the trace line until you have achieved the desired shape.

Using a diamond band saw

With its specially designed diamond-coated stainless steel blade that will cut glass, ceramic tile, and similar hard materials, the band saw has added new dimensions to

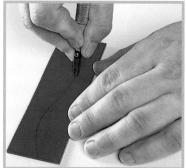

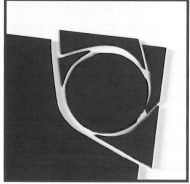

A series of breaks following the arrows on pattern C on pages 12 and 13 will create circular and oval shapes.

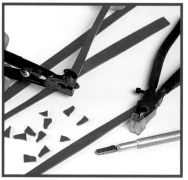

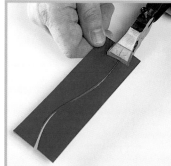

S-shaped curves may require starting runs at each end of the score line so the runs meet near the center.

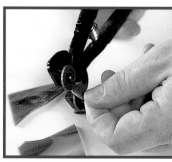

Nippers are one of the most popular tools for making tesserae. The shapes are not always even which is in character with the art of mosaics.

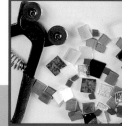

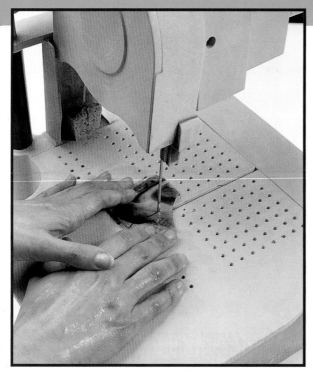

A diamond band saw can cut intricate pattern shapes with smooth edges that do not require grinding.

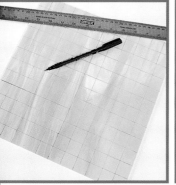
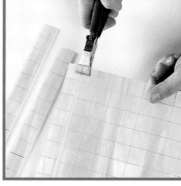

Cutting uniform square tesserae requires making a grid on the glass for the size pieces required and scoring with a glass cutter and a straightedge. Running pliers break the scored lines into strips. Break strips into individual tesserae.

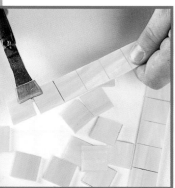
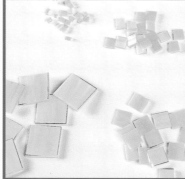

stained glass and mosaic crafting. It can cut intricate pattern shapes and eliminates the need for grinding smooth the edges of the piece. Several models are available at most stained glass retail centers. Read the manufacturer's instructions carefully and follow all safety precautions. The band saw has a water reservoir to cool the blade and prevent glass dust from becoming airborne; therefore, plug the saw into a grounded electrical outlet to avoid shocks.

1 Trace the pattern shape onto the glass or tile with a metallic paint marker or a thin-line paint marker and allow to dry thoroughly before cutting so water won't wash away the outline. Or make a copy of pattern piece from a clear overhead transparency sheet and secure it to the glass or tile surface with double-sided tape.

2 Place water in the reservoir and have a moistened sponge positioned adjacent to the diamond-coated blade at all times.

3 Cut along the pattern line (following the instructions provided by the manufacturer). Allow space between each mosaic piece for the application of cement and/or grout.

4 Rinse each piece under clear running water to remove grit.

NOTE   Always wear safety glasses when using any glass cutting or breaking tool.

Making stained glass tesserae

Many square or rectangular tesserae of colored glass can be used to fill in areas of a mosaic project. Make stained glass tesserae using one of these methods.

Cutting uniform tesserae (Method 1)

1 Cut a piece of glass 12 in by 12 in making sure edges are square.

2 Align a ruler along one side of the sheet of glass and make a mark on the edge of the glass at every 1 in interval.

3 Repeat step 2 on each of the four sides of the glass sheet.

4 Align a cork-backed straightedge along the marks on two opposing sides and score a straight line at each 1 in interval with a glass cutter.

5 Repeat step 4 for the remaining two opposing sides. There should be a grid work of score lines visible on the surface of the glass.

6 With a pair of running pliers, break the score lines along one side, creating strips 1 in wide by 12 in long.

7 Take each strip and break the remaining score lines. There should now be 144 pieces of 1 in sq tesserae.

NOTE   To vary amounts and sizes of tesserae, adjust the

size of the glass sheet and the scoring intervals.

Cutting random-size tesserae (Method 2)

1 With a glass cutter, randomly score lines from one edge of a small sheet of glass to the opposing side. Vary the width between each score line while keeping the score lines no wider than 1 in apart.

2 Repeat step 1 for the remaining two opposing sides.

3 With running pliers, break the score lines along one side, creating long narrow strips.

4 Take each strip and break the remaining score lines into individual, random-size pieces.

NOTE Alternatively, cut narrow strips of glass and nip the strips into smaller pieces with glass mosaic cutters.

Cutting and shaping tesserae, chinaware, and tiles

There are a variety of tools and techniques that can be used to produce individual pieces of a mosaic. Always wear safety glasses and a work apron when cutting or shaping any mosaic material. Use a china marker to indicate where pieces need to be trimmed as a permanent marker may stain some porous materials.

Hammer One swift hit with an ordinary carpenter's hammer will quickly reduce a piece of chinaware or a ceramic tile into many smaller segments. Place the object into a sturdy bag or an old pillowcase before hitting to contain shards and flying debris.

Tile nippers Tile nippers are a plier-like tool with tungsten carbide jaws that cut clay-based materials for mosaic work.

Cutting into smaller sections

1 Grip the tile nippers in your writing hand and hold the tile, glazed side up, in the opposite hand.

2 Position the tile between the jaws of the nippers overlapping the tile edge approximately ⅛ in. The jaws should be perpendicular to the tile edge.

3 Using a scissor-like motion, squeeze the handles together in a single firm motion and snap the tile into two pieces.

Cutting a specific size and shape

1 Use a china marker to mark the shape to be cut from the tile.

2 Using the above technique, nibble small portions of tile to achieve desired shape.

Glass cutter Use this tool (p11) to score some tile and

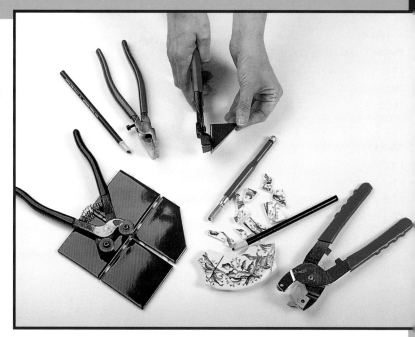

Tesserae can be cut and shaped with tile nippers, glass cutter, snap cutter, or wet saw. When using tile nippers, the mosaic material should not be inside the jaws more than ⅛ in.

ceramic materials, cut curves into tiles, or break chinaware into smaller segments.

1 Score the tile along the cut to be made on glazed side of piece.

2 Score a grid of lines on the section of material to be removed. Use tile nippers to remove unwanted small bits, one piece at a time.

NOTE Jaws of tile nippers should overlap the edge of the piece only ⅛ in and run parallel to the score lines.

Snap cutter Use this tool to make a series of straight cuts on a single tile or cut quantities of tile quickly:

1 Using a china marker, mark where tile cut is to be made and position it on the metal frame of the cutter.

2 Align the carbide-tipped cutter wheel or blade along the marked line. Using a light but steady pressure, score the tile by drawing the cutter wheel along the top of the tile in one even stroke.

3 Press down on the cutter handle to break the tile into two pieces along the scored line.

Mini-cutter Designed to cut smaller tiles, a mini-cutter has a carbide steel cutting wheel at its head and plier-like handles to snap the tile in two.

1 With the glazed or smoothest side of the tile facing upward, score the tile with a single motion.

2 Placing the scored tile in the jaws of the cutter, position tile with the score line facing up and centered on the lower jaw.

3 Squeeze handles together to break the tile along the score line.

Wet saw   This stationary circular saw equipped with a water-cooled abrasive blade can cut large quantities of tiles requiring straight cuts. Wet saws can be rented from home and garden centers, hardware stores, or flooring centers. Many centers will cut tile for a fee. Read the instructions carefully and follow all safety precautions outlined by the manufacturer.

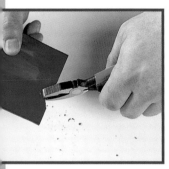

Jagged edges of glass can be smoothed by grozing.

Below left   Keep carborundum stone or diamond pad wet at all times when smoothing sharp edges. Rinse away glass residue when finished.

Below right   File away the jagged edge holding the tool at a slight angle.

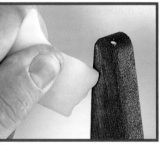 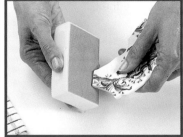

Use a glass grinder to swipe along the edges of the glass to take away any sharp edges. Check each piece against the pattern and mark areas needing further grinding.

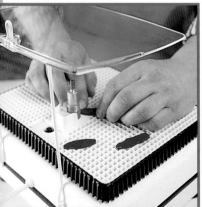 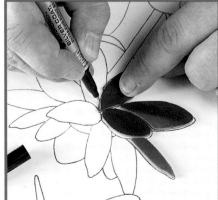

Smoothing jagged and sharp edges on mosaic pieces

The fun of creating a mosaic is that its pieces usually do not need to fit the pattern as precisely as is required for stained glass windows. Stained glass hobbyists and artisans use glass grinders, a carborundum stone, wet/dry sandpaper, or a diamond pad to smooth sharp edges or shape pieces to fit the pattern. If a shape is too difficult to contour, simply alter pattern to accommodate the shape you can achieve.

Grozing   Grasp the piece of glass firmly in one hand, place the combination pliers perpendicular to the edge of the glass, and drag the serrated jaws along the jagged edge in an up-and-down motion. Repeat until the edge is smooth.

Using a carborundum stone, diamond pad, or wet/dry sandpaper   A carborundum stone is a thin rectangular block composed of a hard carbon compound and silicon. Wet/dry sandpaper comes in many grit sizes, is much smoother to the touch than regular sandpapers, is dark gray in color, and can be cut into smaller pieces and/or attached to a sanding block for easier handling. Purchase at hardware stores. Diamond pads can be obtained at some lapidary shops, tile and flooring centers, or glass stores.

1 Wet the smoothing device and the mosaic piece with water. They must be wet at all times to help keep minute glass and clay particles and dust from becoming airborne.

2 Rub the device in a file-like motion and at a slight angle along the edge of the mosaic piece that requires smoothing.

3 Rinse the piece and the device under running water to clean.

Using a glass grinder

1 Attach a face shield to the grinder and position a back splash along the back and sides of the grinder to contain airborne glass chips and water overspray.

2 Keep water in the reservoir and have a moistened sponge positioned adjacent to the diamond-coated bit at all times.

3 Cut each glass piece on the inside of the pattern line so it will fit the pattern with a minimum of grinding and allow cement or grout to fit between each piece. If glass pieces fit the pattern but have sharp edges, make one quick swipe against the grinding bit on each edge of the glass to dull any sharpness. Only light pressure is required.

4 If traces of the marked line are still visible on the piece, grind the edge to ensure an accurate fit within the pattern lines.

5 Check each piece against the pattern. If any part of the piece overlaps and there is not adequate spacing between the pattern pieces, mark the area with a permanent waterproof marker and grind away the excess.

6 Rinse each piece under clear running water when grinding is complete.

7 To ensure proper performance of the glass grinder, clean thoroughly and rinse the water reservoir after each use. NOTE   Remove small chips along a ground edge with a diamond-coated mirror grinding bit that has a groove that grinds the edges of the glass at several angles, providing a smoother finish.

Mosaic Construction Techniques

Two traditional mosaic techniques are used to construct the projects in this book, the direct method and the indirect (or reverse) method.

Direct method   Each tessera is positioned and secured directly to the base/support structure with an adhesive, allowed to set, and then grouted. This method is used for free-form work, when mosaic materials are not consistent in size, shape, and thickness, or when the base structure is a three-dimensional object. The project can be viewed as it develops and changed to use other mosaic pieces for play of light and texture.

Indirect (or reverse) method   provides a smoother, more level surface. The tesserae are arranged face down and adhered to a sheet of clear adhesive-backed vinyl that is positioned over a reversed copy of the pattern. A thin layer of adhesive is applied to the base/support structure and the sheet of vinyl with the attached tesserae is then turned over and applied to the adhesive. Once the adhesive has set, the vinyl is removed and the mosaic is ready for grouting. A variation of the indirect method is also used for garden and patio stone projects where tesserae-covered vinyl is placed at the bottom of a mold or form and topped with cement. The mosaic is revealed once the cement has hardened and the garden stone is released from the mold.

Direct Method
Basic steps
The materials and tools required will vary for each mosaic project. This comprehensive list covers all projects.

Materials
2 copies of pattern
Base/support structure for mosaic
Carbon paper
Masking tape
Newspaper
Mosaic materials for project—art glass, chinaware, vitreous glass tiles, glass nuggets, marbles and jewels, ceramic tiles, found objects, etc.
Dish soap and water
Tile adhesive
Paper cup
Tile grout
Water
Sealants (optional)

Tools
Apron
Safety glasses
Utility knife
Hard-tipped pen or pencil
Permanent waterproof fine-tipped marker and/or china marker
Cork-backed straightedge
Glass cutter
Tile and/or glass mosaic nippers
Running pliers
Breaking/grozing pliers
Smoothing device—carborundum stone, wet/dry sandpaper, diamond pad, or glass grinder
Small containers or jars
Craft stick or small palette knife
Tweezers and/or dental tools
Paint scraper
Small container for mixing grout
Respirator or dust mask
Rubber or latex gloves
Sponge
Soft lint-free cloth
Soft bristled brushes and/or toothbrush

Preparing the pattern

1 Make 2 copies (p10) of the pattern.

2 Verify that outline of pattern fits within the area on the base/support structure that is to be covered with tesserae. Adjust pattern copies if alterations are required.

3 Use one pattern copy as a guide for cutting, breaking, and shaping the mosaic pieces to correct size and shape. Use second copy to cut out any pattern piece that needs a template (opaque materials) remembering to cut *inside* the pattern lines.

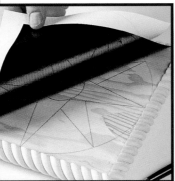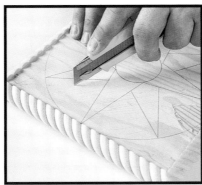

After verifying that the pattern fits properly, transfer the pattern onto the base/support structure using carbon paper. The surface of the base/support structure must be roughened to ensure that adhesives will hold the tesserae to the structure.

Preparing the base/support structure

1 Clean base/support structure surface to remove any dust, oil, wax, or grease. Glass, glazed ceramic, and other non-porous structures should not require further preparation.

2 Smooth rough edges (use sandpaper or carpenter's file to remove ragged edges on wood structures and terra-cotta pots).

Sealants

Apply an appropriate sealant if necessary (consult a local tiling expert for advice).

Interior settings Most projects in this book that are based on a ¾ in exterior grade plywood base/support structure do not require sealing. A thinner, more porous wood can be sealed on all sides by brushing on a thin coating of wood sealant or a mixture of 50% all-purpose white glue and 50% water. Allow to dry completely before applying adhesive and tesserae. Permanent installations in bathrooms and kitchens are exposed to more moisture and need specific treatment.

Exterior settings Outdoor mosaics should be protected from climate variations by sealing all sides of any wood base structure with a waterproofing agent (silicone-based sealant and compatible water-resistant adhesives and grout). Use a thin-set mortar and grout on concrete surfaces.

Terra-cotta If terra-cotta container is not glazed on the inside, apply a water-resistant silicone sealant to the inside or put the plant and soil into a smaller plastic pot and insert into container. Store containers in dry, protected location during cold weather.

Transferring the pattern onto the base/support structure

1 Place a sheet of carbon paper over the area to be covered with tesserae. Trim to fit and fasten with masking tape.

2 Position pattern copy on top of carbon and fasten with masking tape.

3 Use a hard-tipped pen or pencil to trace pattern.

4 If base where tesserae are to be adhered is wood, key (rough up) the surface by scoring with a utility knife. Small cuts into the wood surface will be sufficient—do not gouge the wood.

Preparing the mosaic pieces

1 Store cut and shaped (pp16–20) tesserae pieces in small containers according to size and color, until ready for use.

2 Trace (p10) any distinctive pieces onto art glass or ceramic material and cut (p11) each piece as required (inside marker line).

3 Smooth and shape as necessary (pp16–20).

4 Clean each piece thoroughly, rinse, and dry.

5 Apply ceramic tile sealant to unglazed and porous tesserae surfaces.

Adhering mosaic pieces to the base/support structure

1 Protect areas that are not to be covered with adhesive or grout with masking tape.

2 Choose a ceramic tile adhesive that is appropriate for the project. For outdoor mosaics choose a thin-set mortar or water-resistant adhesive containing a latex polymer additive for additional strength, flexibility, and water resistance.

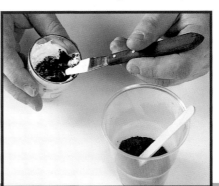

3 If adhesive color differs from grout, mix in a bit of grout to tint adhesive.

Adhesive may ooze from beneath the tesserae. Mix a bit of grout color with the adhesive to make the oozing less noticeable.

4 Put a small amount of pre-mixed adhesive into a paper cup and replenish as needed. Keep lid on large container.

5 Using a small trowel or palette knife, spread a thin layer of adhesive onto a small area that can be covered with tesserae in 15 minutes. Avoid obscuring pattern lines.

6 With a craft stick or palette knife, apply (butter) a thin coat of adhesive to the back of a tessera.

7 Firmly press tessera onto base/support structure in correct position, and twist back and forth slightly to embed in the adhesive. Only minimum oozing should take place.

8 Begin placing tesserae with distinctive shapes and the main design elements first. Applying tesserae color by color helps to avoid placement mistakes.

9 Fill in background of project with remaining tesserae until all areas of mosaic pattern have been covered. Where background has same tesserae apply a slightly thicker layer of adhesive directly onto base and press tesserae firmly in place.

10 Use tweezers, dental pick, or utility knife to reposition pieces, if needed.

11 Allow adhesive to set for 24 hours.

12 Remove any adhesive on mosaic surface with a utility knife or paint scraper.

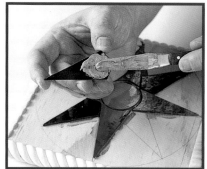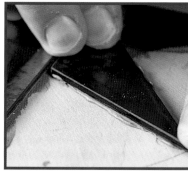

Butter main elements of the piece. Pressing down firmly will cause some adhesive to ooze out around the piece. Apply adhesive directly onto base when adhering a large quantity of the same tesserae at one time.

Applying the grout

Select sanded or non-sanded grout. Sanded grout is grittier and used for filling wider spaces between tesserae, certain outdoor projects, and terra-cotta pots. Non-sanded grouts have a smooth finish and are used for grouting mosaics with narrower spaces between the tesserae, usually indoor projects. This grout shrinks so additional coats may be necessary. Choose water-resistant grouts for finished pieces that are to be left outdoors.

1 Follow manufacturer's instructions, mix required amounts of grout and clean, cool water to a stiff, creamy consistency.

2 Let moist grout stand for 10 minutes, then re-stir, before applying to the mosaic.

3 Wipe a clean, moist sponge across surface of mosaic to slightly dampen tesserae to prevent excessive grout from sticking to their surfaces.

Three methods of applying background fill

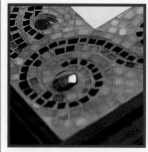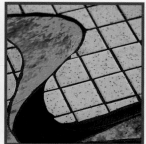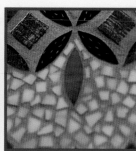

Opus vermiculatum
Tesserae are positioned following the outline of glass pieces already laid. This allows images and lines in the pattern to be accentuated and creates some interesting effects.

Opus tesselatum
Similarly sized and shaped tesserae are applied in rows, both horizontally and vertically, in a grid pattern to form an unobtrusive background for the main features of the mosaic.

Random
As the term implies, the pieces are various sizes and shapes and are placed randomly to fill the background area of the mosaic.

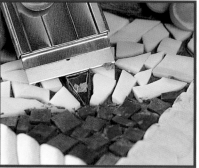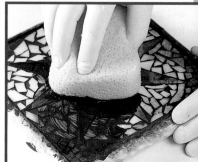

Allow adhesive to set for 24 hours. Use a utility knife to remove adhesive on top of tesserae. Be careful not to scratch surface.

The consistency of the grout is very important—not too runny, but not too stiff. Use gloved hand to gently work the grout between the glass pieces. Wipe excess grout off the surface with a damp sponge.

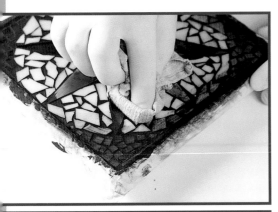

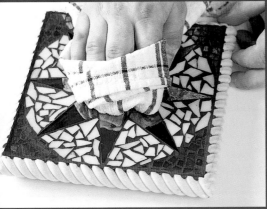

Use a soft cloth to buff the cleaned surface of the mosaic.

Indirect (reverse) Method
Basic Steps

3 copies of pattern

Base/support structure for mosaics

Masking tape

Clear adhesive-backed vinyl

Newspaper

Mosaic pieces for project

Dish soap and water

Tile adhesive

Cardboard

Clear glass sheet

Flat wooden block

Tile grout

Water

Sealants (optional)

Apron

Safety glasses

Light box (optional)

Permanent waterproof fine-tipped marker and/or china marker

Cork-backed straightedge

Glass cutter

Tile and/or glass mosaic nippers

Running pliers

Breaking/grozing pliers

Smoothing device—carborundum stone, wet/dry sandpaper, diamond pad, or glass grinder

Small containers or jars

Craft stick or small palette knife

Tweezers and/or dental tools

Utility knife

Trowel

Hammer or mallet

Paint scraper

Respirator or dust mask

Rubber or latex gloves

Sponge

Soft lint-free cloth

Soft bristled brushes and/or toothbrush

4 With gloved hand or a damp sponge, apply grout to mosaic surface. Gently work it between tesserae until grout is flush with surface and all crevices are filled.

5 Use sponge to wipe off excess grout and level top of grouted areas. Allow the grout to set 15 minutes.

6 Rinse sponge in cool, clean water, wring out excess, and wipe mosaic surface clean.

7 Allow to dry for approximately 40 minutes. A dry haze will be apparent on mosaic surface. Polish with a dry, lint-free cloth.

8 To aid in the curing process, mist with water several times a day or cover with a damp cloth or sheet of plastic. Grout requires a minimum of 24 hours to cure.

Cleaning the finished piece

Remove excess grout by buffing with a soft cloth, or use a paint scraper or utility knife. Remove any masking tape.

Grout sealants

Use a sealant to protect grout where water resistance is needed, such as a mosaic tabletop or a terra-cotta planter. Follow the manufacturer's instructions.

Preparing the pattern

1 Make 3 copies (p10) of pattern.

2 Verify that outline of pattern fits within area on object to be covered with tesserae. Make adjustments as necessary.

3 Use one copy as a guide for cutting, breaking, and shaping mosaic pieces. Use second copy to cut out any pattern piece that requires a template (cut *inside* the pattern lines). Use third copy to place beneath the clear adhesive-backed vinyl to guide the positioning of tesserae.

4 On a light box, place a pattern copy face down and trace the design lines onto the reverse side with the permanent marker. If a light box is not available, tape pattern onto a window (design facing outward), using daylight to illuminate lines to be traced.

5 Tape pattern copy to a flat work surface or board, with the reverse side facing upward.

6 Peel the paper backing from a piece of clear adhesive-backed vinyl that is approximately ½ in larger on each side than the project pattern. Position the vinyl over the pattern taped to work surface, with adhesive side facing up. *Do not stick it to the pattern!* The vinyl should be centered so that ½ in overlaps the pattern on each side. The pattern should be completely covered by the vinyl yet visible through it. Tape in place, but do not position tape within pattern outline.

NOTE   Use clear 8mm sandblast resist material for its thick vinyl and strong adhesive. It is available at most stained glass shops. Or use clear contact paper, but it's not as strong or as adhesive.

Preparing the base/support structure

1 Follow the instructions for Preparing the Base/Support Structure given in the Direct Method (p21).

2 Using the pattern as a guide, mark the outline of the overall mosaic shape onto the base/support structure.

3 If base/support structure is constructed of wood, key (score with a utility knife) the surface, where the tesserae are to be adhered.

Preparing the mosaic pieces

Follow instructions for Preparing the Mosaic Pieces given in the Direct Method (p21). NOTE   Each piece must be cleaned thoroughly to ensure proper adhesion to the clear adhesive-backed vinyl.

Placing the mosaic pieces onto the vinyl

The tesserae are now ready for placement onto the clear adhesive-backed vinyl. Remember, the pattern copy under

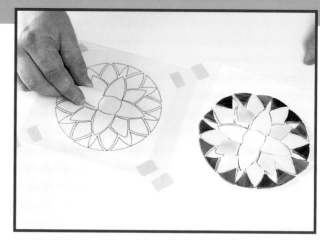

The adhesive-backed vinyl should be larger than the pattern. Position over pattern, adhesive side up. Tape pattern and vinyl to work surface.

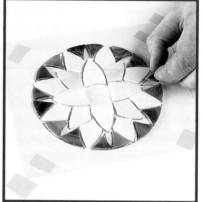
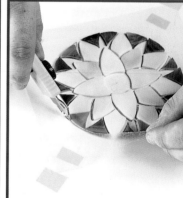

Place the main elements of the mosaic first. Fill in the background last. Trim away excess vinyl when all pieces are down.

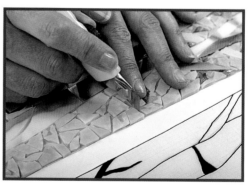

For ease of handling, split large patterns into sections prior to applying to the base/support structure.

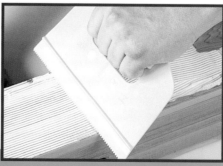

Adhesive is applied with a trowel in the Indirect Method.

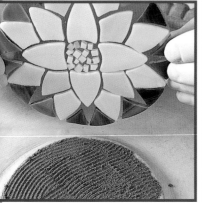

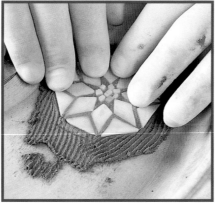

the vinyl is the reverse of the pattern used to cut and shape the individual pieces.

1 Starting with the main design elements in the project foreground, turn each piece of the mosaic over and place face down onto the vinyl in the correct position. Press the pieces firmly onto the resist.

2 Fill in the background of the project with the remaining tesserae until all areas of the project pattern have been covered.

3 Use tweezers, dental pick, or utility knife to remove and reposition pieces, as necessary, but remember repeated lifting can deteriorate the adhesive.

4 Using a utility knife, cut along the outside of the pattern outline, removing excess vinyl.

5 For sizable projects, splitting the mosaic piece into several sections will make application to the base easier. Being careful not to dislodge any glass pieces, run the blade of the utility knife between the glass pieces and cut the vinyl underneath. Separate into sections as required.

For smaller sections, align one edge of the mosaic section with the corresponding pattern edge. Turn vinyl over and place pieces onto the adhesive.

Applying the adhesive

1 Follow steps 1 to 3 from Adhering the Mosaic Pieces to the Base/Support Structure, (p21).

2 Using a notched trowel, apply a thin, even layer of adhesive to the base where the mosaic is to be applied. Try not to cover the outside pattern line which acts as the guide for applying the mosaic.

Applying the mosaic

1 The trick to the indirect method is turning over the sections of mosaic that are adhered to the vinyl without dislodging the tesserae and then applying it to the base in the correct position.

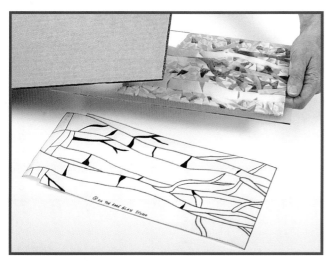

For larger sections, sandwich the mosaic between a sheet of glass and cardboard to turn the pieces over. Align the mosaic over the base and carefully pull the glass sheet from beneath the mosaic.

Smaller mosaic sections can be put in place by following these steps.

A   With the base close at hand, gently lift the mosaic-laden vinyl.

B   Align one edge of the mosaic section with the corresponding pattern edge.

C   Carefully turn the vinyl over and place the mosaic pieces onto the adhesive. Check that the mosaic section is correctly positioned and press into place.

Larger mosaic sections can be accurately applied without dislodging pieces from the vinyl by following these steps.

A   Carefully slide the mosaic-laden vinyl onto a piece of cardboard and place a clear glass sheet (at least 3mm thick)

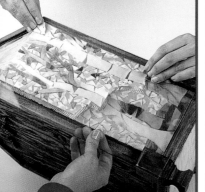

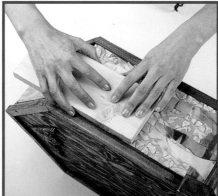

A flat wood block firmly presses glass in place. Allow adhesive to set for 24 hours. Then carefully peel away the vinyl backing.

on top. Both cardboard and glass sheet must be slightly larger than the mosaic section.

B   Holding the layers tightly together, turn the mosaic section over so that the clear glass sheet is on the bottom. Remove the top cardboard layer.

C   Align the mosaic section with two adjacent edges of the glass sheet. Holding the glass sheet over the base/support structure, line up edges of the mosaic section with the area where it is to be applied. The glass sheet must not be touching the adhesive.

D   Grasp the edges of the vinyl. With the aid of a helper, slowly pull the clear glass sheet out from beneath the mosaic. Press the mosaic firmly to the adhesive. Repeat for each mosaic section to be adhered. Align the section so that a visible seam or division does not exist between the sections—the mosaic should look like one unit.

2   Do not remove vinyl at this stage. Some mosaic pieces may come away with the vinyl if it is peeled off before the adhesive has set.

3   Using a flat wooden block and a hammer or mallet, gently tamp each section down onto the adhesive until firmly in place.

4   Allow adhesive to set completely for 24 hours or as recommended by the adhesive manufacturer.

5   Remove vinyl, exposing the top surface of the mosaic. Use a utility knife or paint scraper to remove any adhesive on the surface of the mosaic, taking care not to scratch the tesserae.

Applying the grout, cleaning the finished piece, and grout sealants

Follow the same instructions for these final stages as provided in the Direct Method (pp22, 23).

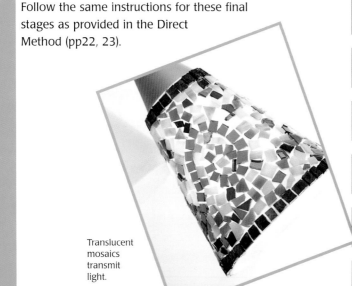

Translucent mosaics transmit light.

Translucent Mosaics
Basic Steps

Translucent mosaics differ from traditional mosaics by transmitting light through the tesserae instead of reflecting it from the surface of the mosaic pieces. Colors and textures are illuminated from within. Luminous window hangings, lamps, and sculptural objects are an exciting new dimension to the art of mosaics.

Materials

2 copies of pattern
Translucent base/support structure for mosaic
Mosaic materials for project—art glass, glass nuggets, marbles, jewels, found objects, etc.
Newspaper
Dish soap and water
Masking tape
Clear silicone adhesive
Disposable cup
Isopropyl (rubbing) alcohol
Tile grout
Water

Tools

Apron
Safety glasses
Utility knife or scissors
Permanent waterproof fine-tipped marker
Cork-backed straightedge
Glass cutter
Tile and/or glass mosaic nippers
Running pliers
Breaking/grozing pliers
Smoothing device—carborundum stone, wet/dry sandpaper, diamond pad, or glass grinder
Small containers or jars
Caulking gun
Small palette knife or craft stick
Tweezers and/or dental pick
Paint scraper
Small container for mixing grout
Respirator or dust mask
Rubber or latex gloves
Sponge
Soft lint-free cloth
Soft bristled brushes and/or toothbrush

Preparing the pattern

1 Make 2 copies (p10) of the pattern.

2 Verify that the outline of the pattern fits within the area to be covered on the base/support structure. Adjust the pattern copies if any alterations have been made to the original pattern.

3 Use one copy as a guide for cutting, breaking, and shaping the mosaic pieces to the correct size and shape. When cutting materials through which the pattern lines are not clearly visible, cut out a template for the required pieces from the second pattern copy, remembering to cut *inside* the pattern lines.

Preparing the base/support structure

The purpose of a translucent mosaic is to allow light to pass through and illuminate the individual tesserae rather than have light reflecting off the surface. Silicone is a powerful adhesive that becomes quite transparent once it has cured and is ideally suited to adhering glass tesserae to smooth, non-porous surfaces. To further inhibit the eye from recognizing the use of an adhesive, choose a textured art glass that has an interesting texture while still allowing light to pass through it.

1 Smooth rough edges or surfaces with the

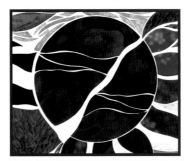

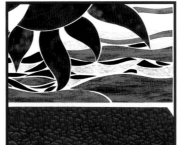

appropriate tools or materials.

2 Use dish soap and water to clean the surface of the base/support structure, removing any trace of dust, oil, wax, or grease. Glass and other non-porous structures should not require any further preparation.

Preparing the mosaic pieces

1 For patterns that require a stated quantity of tesserae of the same size and shape, cut and/or shape the tesserae (p17) as described and sort into small jars or containers, according to size and color.

2 Most translucent mosaic projects utilize art glass, cut and shaped into distinctive configurations. Using a waterproof marker and a pattern copy as a guide, trace (pp10, 11) each piece onto the material to be cut.

3 Cut (pp10, 11) each piece as required, cutting inside the marker line.

4 Smooth and shape any jagged edge (p19). Shape the pieces to fit within the pattern lines. This leaves the necessary space required if the mosaic is to be grouted.

5 Clean each piece thoroughly to ensure adhesion to the base. Remove all traces of cutter oil, marker, grinding residue, etc. with soap and water. Rinse thoroughly with clean water.

Adhering the mosaic pieces to the base/support structure

The application of tesserae for a translucent mosaic is a variation of the Direct Method (p20).

1 Before adhering tesserae to the base/support structure, protect any areas that are not to be covered with adhesive or grout with masking tape.

2 Use masking tape to secure a pattern copy to the work surface. Align the base piece over the pattern into the correct position.

3 Place the tube of silicone into a caulking gun and squeeze a small amount of silicone out of the tube and into a disposable cup or a smaller container. Because silicone starts to set or harden once exposed to air, reseal the tube and replenish the supply of silicone only as needed.

4 Using a small palette knife or craft stick, spread a thin layer of adhesive onto the base in a small area that can be covered with tesserae in approximately 15 minutes. Use just enough silicone to bond the tesserae to the surface of the base so that on placement the silicone does not ooze out. If

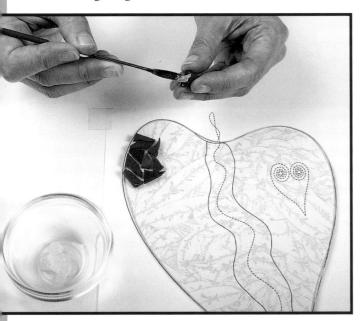

Tape pattern copy to work surface and place base piece over top, textured side down.

applied properly, the silicone should be practically invisible once the tesserae are firmly attached to the base. Alternatively, butter the backs of the tesserae with adhesive.

5   When adhering the mosaic pieces, apply the tesserae one section at a time using the pattern beneath the base as your guide. Firmly press a tessera onto the base in the correct position, twisting the piece back and forth slightly, to embed it firmly in the silicone. Use a palette knife or craft stick to remove excess silicone before it sets.

6   If any of the mosaic pieces are not in the correct position, pick up the piece that needs adjusting with the aid of a pair of tweezers, dental pick, or utility knife. Apply additional silicone, only if required, and reset the piece in the mosaic.

7   Allow the silicone to set for at least 24 hours or as recommended by the manufacturer.

8   Use a utility knife or paint scraper to remove any adhesive on the surface of the mosaic, taking care not to scratch the tesserae. A cloth moistened with isopropyl (rubbing) alcohol will remove traces of silicone but care must be taken not to spill the alcohol directly onto the mosaic. The alcohol can compromise the integrity of the silicone bond if it seeps between and under the tesserae.

Applying the grout, cleaning the finished piece, and grout sealants

Follow the same instructions for these final stages as provided in the Direct Method (pp22, 23).

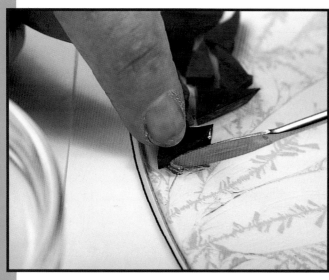

Carefully scrape away adhesive on tesserae with a palette knife before silicone sets.

Base/Support Structures

Almost anything can be used as a base/support structure if the surface is clean and relatively smooth, the appropriate adhesive is used, and the structure can support the weight of the tesserae. Use glass and ceramic containers, vases, plates, and lamp shades or give furniture pieces new life. To create a more permanent mosaic installation, consider a section of floor or a feature wall as the site for your next mosaic project.

Specific information regarding the requirements and the preparation of base/support structures are described in the instructions given for each project in this book.

Making wood base/support structures for mosaic panels and wall hangings

Many mosaic wall hanging and panel projects are constructed on a wood base/support structure. Patterns can be adjusted to accommodate an existing base/support structure or make the base from ¾ in exterior grade plywood. The plywood can support the weight of a mosaic and will rarely warp.

Safety reminder   When operating power tools, read the manufacturer's directions and follow all safety guidelines and precautions. Always wear a work apron and safety glasses.

Materials
1 copy of pattern
¾ in exterior grade plywood
Wood trim molding (at least ¾ in wide)
Carpenter's wood glue
Finishing nails
Wood filler
Sandpaper
Wood stain
Felt or cork pads

Tools
Apron
Safety glasses
Marking pen or pencil
Drawing or carpenter's square
Wood saw (hand or power)
Hammer or air nailer
Applicator brush for wood stain or paint
Soft lint-free cloths for buffing

1 Measure the width and height of the project pattern.

2 With a marking pen or pencil, trace the outline of the base shape onto the plywood sheet. For square and rectangular shapes, use a square and straightedge when drawing the outline.

3 Cut out, using a wood saw.

4 For straight-sided projects requiring a raised edge, cut a length of wood trim molding for each of the sides of the base piece. Each end must be mitered (miter each end of molding for square and rectangular projects at a 45° angle) at the corners to maintain a finished appearance.

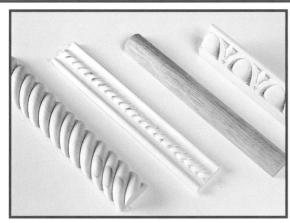

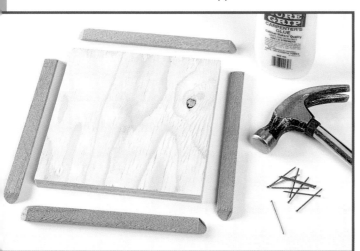

Choose from a wide variety of framing materials to enhance mosaic piece.

5 Apply a bead of carpenter's wood glue to an outside edge of the base piece and place a length of the molding overtop. Fasten the molding to the base piece with a hammer and finishing nails. Repeat this step with the remaining three lengths of trim, making sure that the mitered ends of each length are butted up against the adjacent pieces. The wood trim should be slightly wider than the base to give a finished look and contain the mosaic pieces.

6 Fill nail holes and gaps with wood filler and smooth with sandpaper.

7 Choose a stain or paint that complements the color of grout. Application of the paint or stain to the base/support structure can be done before or after the mosaic has been adhered to the base and the grouting is complete. Do not apply paint or stain to any surface that will hold tesserae.

8 Apply felt or cork pads to the back of the base piece to prevent marring wall or table surfaces.

Mounting wall hangings, plaques, and mirrors

1 Place the wall hanging or mirror face down on the work surface.

2 Make two level marks 4 in from top of piece and 1½ to 2 in from either side.

3 At each of these marks, fasten in screw eye or heavy-duty eyelet to the plywood base. Use ½ in long screws so that they do not go through the ¾ in plywood base and damage front of mosaic.

4 String a double strand of picture hanging wire between the two screws, threading it through the eyes. Wrap the ends of the wire around the strand several times to secure.

5 To hang larger and heavier pieces, drill two holes into the wall in the desired location. Insert the appropriate plugs or anchors, depending on the type of wall surface. Insert and tighten a screw three-quarters of the way into each plug. Suspend the mosaic piece on the wall by hooking the wire onto the two screws. Hang small mosaic pieces directly on wall on a picture hook or small nail.

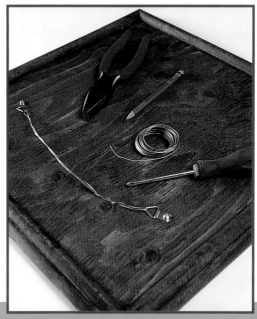

When mounting wall hangings, remember that the mosaic piece will be heavy. Appropriate precautions should be taken to ensure the piece does not fall away from the wall.

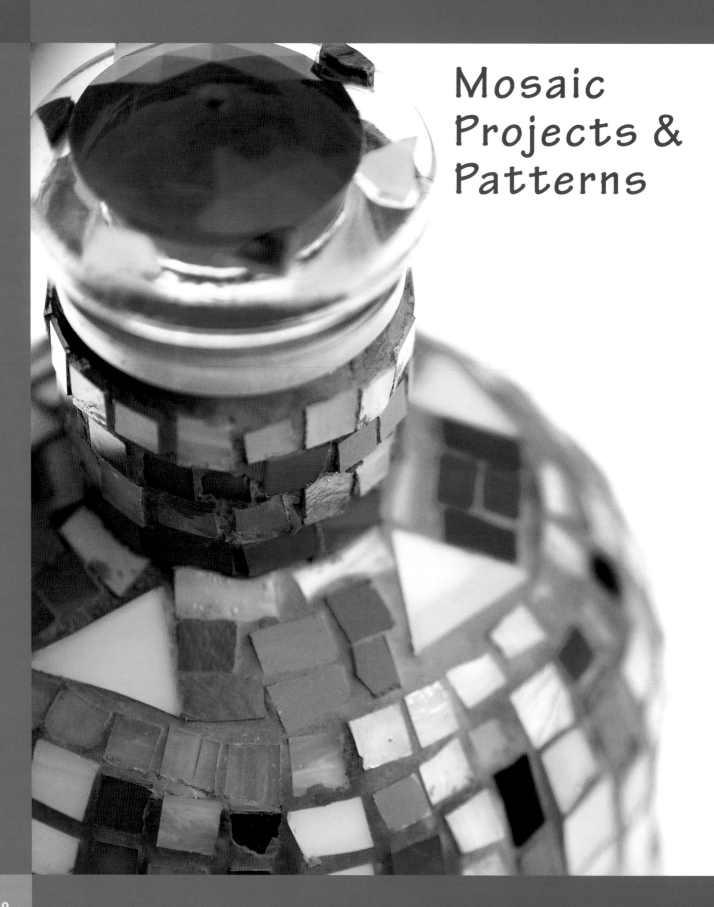

Mosaic Projects & Patterns

Genie Bottle

fancy bottle project—various sizes

Mosaic material required

Approximately 1 sq ft each of assorted translucent and opaque art glasses in vibrant shades of red, orange, blue, green, and purple is required to cover a glass bottle 9 in tall with a circumference of 14 in. Cut the art glasses into square and rectangular tesserae of random sizes (p18) no more than $\frac{1}{2}$ in x $\frac{1}{2}$ in and approximately 10 to 12—1 in wide x $\frac{1}{2}$ in high triangular tesserae. The quantities and types of art glass used can vary depending on the size of vessel, availability of materials, and personal color preferences.

Base/support structure

A glass bottle is the base for this mosaic project. Size is given above, but almost any size or shape of glass or ceramic vessel can be utilized.

Mosaic instructions

Follow basic instructions given for Translucent Mosaics—Basic Steps (p26) to make this mosaic project. Refer to the photograph of the finished mosaic as a potential guide for placement of the various types of tesserae. No pattern is given which allows individual freedom to achieve a more spontaneous and less contrived look, reminiscent of an ancient genie bottle. This order of procedure may be helpful.

1 Adhere tesserae with silicone to achieve a solid bond with the glass bottle.

2 Cap the bottle with a glass stopper covered with glued-on rich, jewel-tone faceted glass gems and small tesserae.

3 Fill the interstices between the tesserae with a purple-tinted non-sanded grout.

NOTE

• Leave $\frac{1}{16}$ in space along the bottom edge of the glass bottle free of tesserae to avoid scratching furniture.

• Use tile or glass mosaic cutters (nippers) to divide large tessera in half and from there into smaller shapes and sizes.

There is no pattern for this mosaic project.

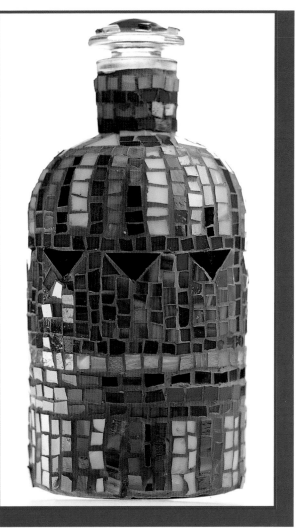

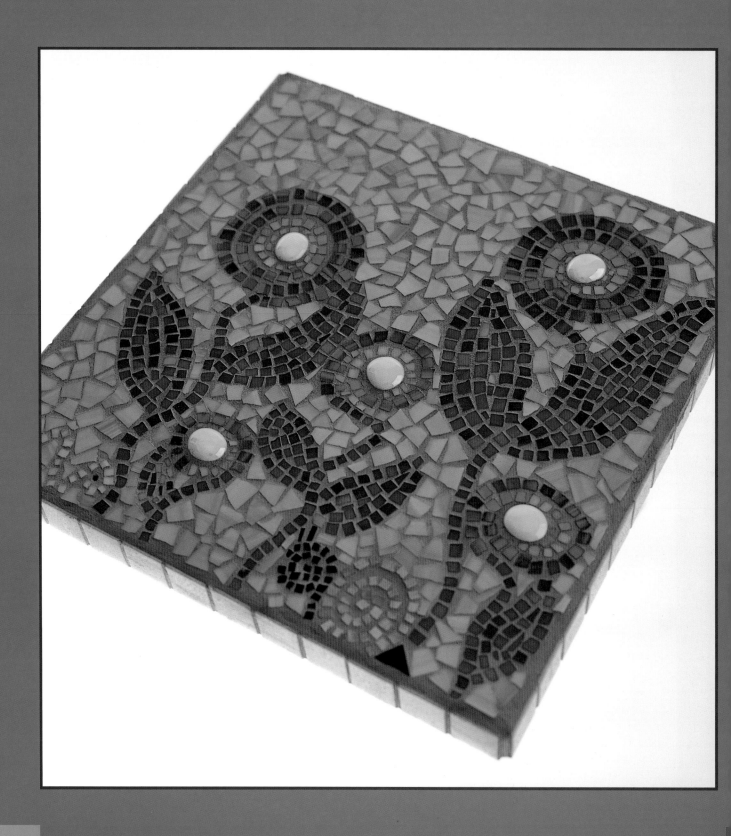

Child's Garden

small wall hanging

Mosaic panel size 10 in square

Mosaic material required

Letters refer to the type and quantity of mosaic material used on pattern pieces (p34).
The quantities and types of materials listed are the minimum requirements for completing this project as illustrated, but materials may be substituted, if desired.

- A 6 in x 8 in opaque blue with white wisps art glass (cut into random-size tesserae)
- B 3 in x 6 in opaque orange with white wisps art glass (cut into ¼ in x ¼ in tesserae)
- C 3 in x 10 in opaque medium green with light green art glass (cut into ¼ in x ¼ in tesserae)
- D 1 in x 2 in opaque lime green art glass (cut into ¼ in x ¼ in tesserae)
- E 1 in x 2 in opaque iridescent gray art glass (cut into ¼ in x ¼ in tesserae)
- F 1 in x 2 in black art glass (cut snail's tail and antennae; cut balance into ¼ in x ¼ in tesserae)
- G 1 in x 1 in opaque red art glass (cut ¼ in x ¼ in tesserae for snail and inchworm eye pieces)
- H 5 iridescent yellow glass nuggets (medium)
- J 48−¾ in x ¾ in leaf green vitreous glass mosaic tiles

NOTE The letter I is not used in this listing.

Base/support structure

1 piece 10 in x 10 in−¾ in exterior grade plywood

Guidelines for constructing a base with wood trim molding are given in Making Wood Base/Support Structures for Mosaic Panels and Wall Hangings (p28).

Mosaic instructions

Fabricate the mosaic panel by following the instructions given for the Direct Method (p20). Refer to the photograph of the finished mosaic as a guide for placement of the various types of tesserae.

1 Begin by placing the center of the flowers (H) on the base/support structure. Continue by applying the flower tesserae (B) in a spiral fashion working outward from the flower centers and progressing to the stem pieces (C).

2 Form the leaves by using the opus vermiculatum method (p22) to apply the tesserae (C). For each leaf, begin by applying a perimeter row of tesserae (C) within the pattern outline. Using a glass cutter or

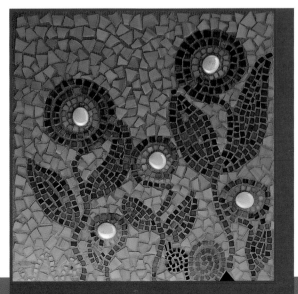

mosaic nippers, trim a tessera to fit into spaces that are not large enough to accommodate a whole piece. When the entire row around the perimeter of a leaf has been adhered, start a new row within the one just completed. Using this method, fill in the remainder of the leaf.

3 Using the pattern lines as a guide, apply the tesserae that comprise the snail (E, F, G) and the inchworm (D, G).

4 Fill in the mosaic background with random-size tesserae (A). Start in the center of the mosaic working your way outward until the mosaic is completely filled in. Leave approximately ¹/₁₆ in perimeter around the mosaic free of

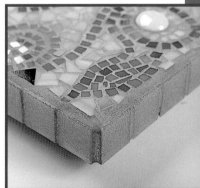

tesserae to ensure that tesserae do not protrude over the edge of the base.

5 With the base lying flat on the work surface adhere the vitreous glass mosaic tiles (J) along the *outside* edge of the plywood. Each of the four sides will require 12 tiles

evenly spaced approximately ¹⁄₁₆ in apart. Allow the adhesive to set for approximately 24 hours.

6 Complete the mosaic by following the instructions for Applying the Grout (p22) and Cleaning the Finished Piece (p23). A soft blue-tinted sanded grout is used to fill the interstices between the tesserae.

7 Refer to Mounting Wall Hangings, Plaques, and Mirrors (p29) for instructions on hanging the finished mosaic.

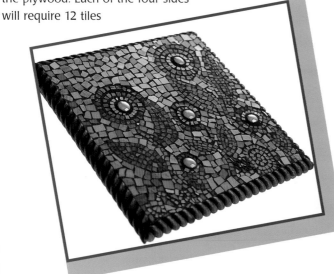

Alternate material selection

A 6 in x 8 in opaque iridescent gray art glass (cut into random-size tesserae)

B 3 in x 6 in opaque purple and opaque iridescent amber art glass (cut into ¼ in x ¼ in tesserae)

C 3 in x 10 in opaque medium green with light green art glass (cut into ¼ in x ¼ in tesserae)

D 1 in x 2 in opaque lime green art glass (cut into ¼ in x ¼ in tesserae)

E 1 in x 2 in opaque pale purple with tan wisps art glass (cut into ¼ in x ¼ in tesserae)

F 1 in x 2 in black art glass (cut snail antennae and inchworm eye pieces; cut balance into ¼ in x ¼ in tesserae)

G 1 in x 2 in opaque brown art glass (cut snail tail; cut balance into ¼ in x ¼ in tesserae)

H 5 iridescent lime green glass nuggets (medium)

NOTE Alternate glass selection project does not use glass tiles for border. *See* photograph.

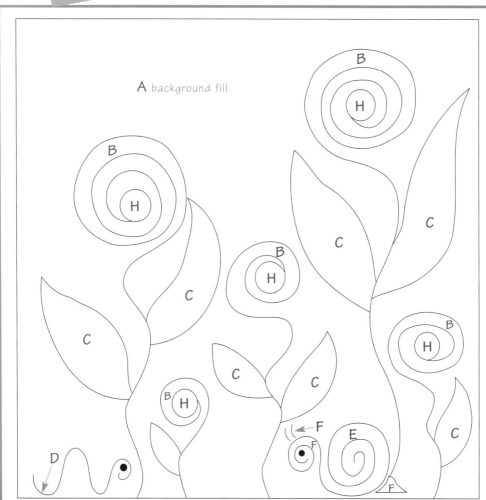

A background fill

C flower stems

G snail & inchworm eyes

Erich's Room

wall plaque

Mosaic panel size   4¾ in wide by 3¼ in high oval

Mosaic material required

Letters refer to the type and quantity of mosaic material used on pattern pieces (p36).
The quantities and types of materials listed are the minimum requirements for completing this project as illustrated, but materials may be substituted, if desired.

A   2 in x 3 in opaque red art glass
B   3 in x 3 in opaque white art glass (cut into medium random-size tesserae)
C   1 in x 3 in opaque iridescent blue art glass (cut into ½ in x ¼ in tesserae)

Base/support structure

5¾ in wide x 4⅛ in high hemlock oval rosette with ¼ in deep recess to accommodate mosaic

Mosaic instructions

This mosaic panel can be fabricated using either the Direct Method (p20) or the Indirect Method (p23) of mosaic construction. Choose the method you prefer.

Adjust the pattern to spell out the child's name you desire as the central motif of this mosaic project. Refer to the photograph of the finished mosaic as a guide for placement of the various types of tesserae.

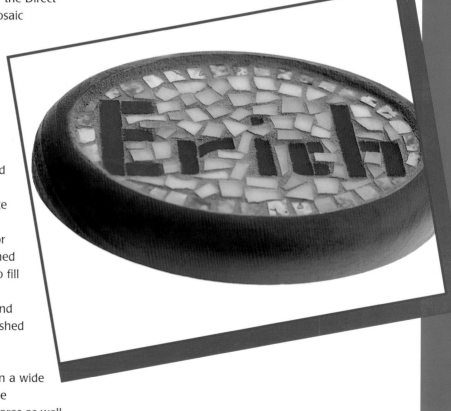

1   Cut (pp11, 14–18) required tesserae pieces and adhere tesserae (A) to form child's name and border tesserae (C).
2   Fill in background of mosaic with random-size opaque white tesserae (B).
3   Complete mosaic by following instructions for Applying the Grout (p22) and Cleaning the Finished Piece (p23). A blue-tinted sanded grout is used to fill the interstices between the tesserae.
4   Refer to Mounting Wall Hangings, Plaques, and Mirrors (p29) for instructions on hanging the finished mosaic.

NOTE
Ready-made architectural fixtures are available in a wide variety of sizes, shapes, and materials and can be purchased at craft, department, and hardware stores as well as the local home and garden center. The small hemlock oval rosette used for this wall plaque project is a perfect size to work on while you practice various mosaic techniques.

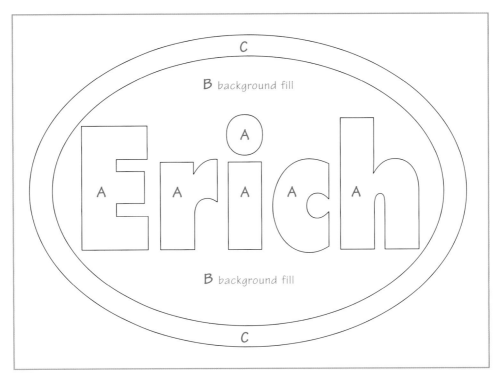

C

B background fill

A

A A A A A

B background fill

C

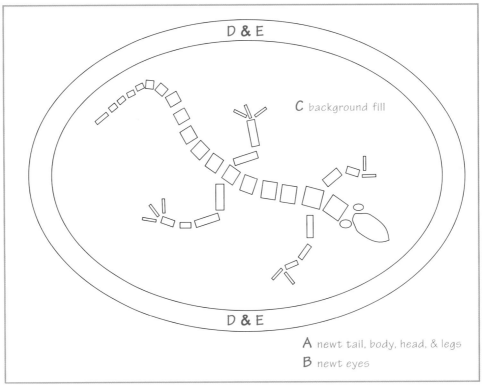

D & E

C background fill

D & E

A newt tail, body, head, & legs

B newt eyes

Hannah's Newt

wall plaque

Mosaic panel size   4¾ in wide by 3¼ in high oval

Mosaic material required

Letters refer to the type and quantity of mosaic material used on pattern pieces (p36).
The quantities and types of materials listed are the minimum requirements for completing this
project as illustrated, but materials may be substituted, if desired.

    A   2 in x 3 in blue and green ring mottle art glass
    B   1 in x 1 in opaque brown art glass (cut into small random-size tesserae)
    C   3 in x 3 in opaque ivory art glass (cut into small random-size tesserae)
    D   1 in x 3 in opaque lime green art glass (cut into ¼ in x ¼ in tesserae)
    E   1 in x 1 in mirrored light amber semi-antique art glass (cut into small random-size
        tesserae)

Base/support structure

5¾ in wide x 4⅛ in high hemlock oval rosette with ¼ in
deep recess to accommodate mosaic

Mosaic instructions

This mosaic panel can be fabricated using either the Direct
Method (pp20-23) or the Indirect Method (pp23-26) of
mosaic construction. Choose the method you prefer to work
with. Refer to the photograph of the finished mosaic as a
guide for placement of the various types of tesserae.

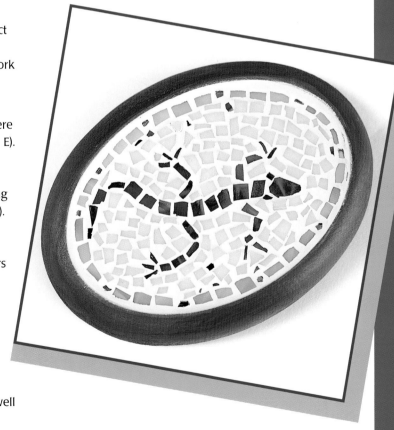

1 Cut (pp11, 14-18) all required tesserae pieces and adhere
tesserae (A, B) to form newt body and border tesserae (D, E).

2 Fill in background of mosaic with random-size ivory
tesserae (C).

3 Complete mosaic by following instructions for Applying
the Grout (pp22-23) and Cleaning the Finished Piece (p23).
An ivory-tinted non-sanded grout is used to fill the
interstices between the tesserae.

4 Refer to Mounting Wall Hangings, Plaques, and Mirrors
(p29) for instructions on hanging the finished mosaic.

NOTE

• Liven up the monotone ivory tesserae (C) used in the
mosaic background by interspersing the occasional
brown tessera (B).

• Ready-made architectural fixtures are available in a
wide variety of sizes, shapes, and materials and can be
purchased at craft, department, and hardware stores as well
as the local home and garden center. The small hemlock
oval rosette used for this wall plaque project is the perfect
size to work on while practicing various mosaic techniques.

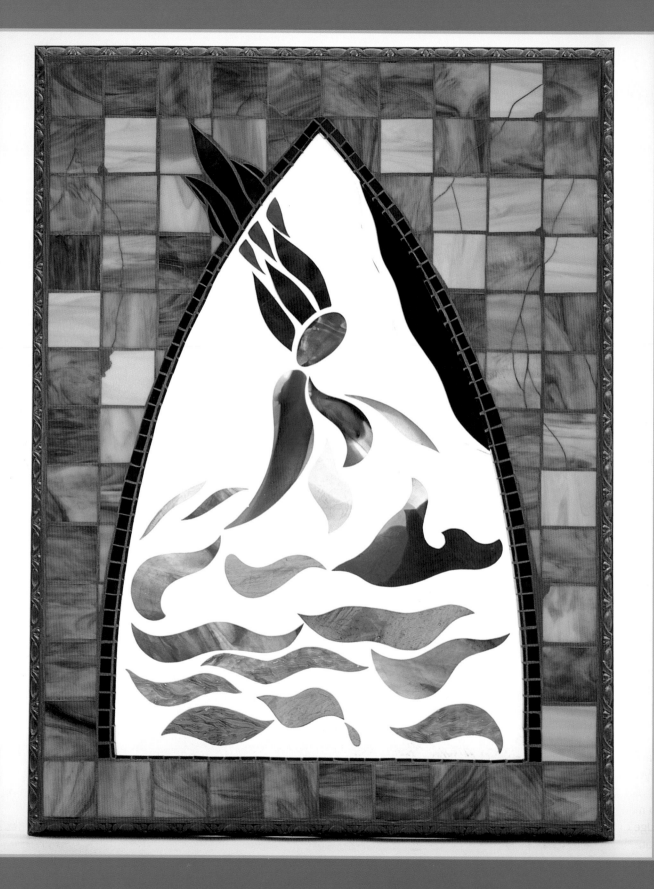

Aquarius

translucent window hanging

Mosaic panel size   19½ in wide by 25⅝ in high

Mosaic material required

Letters refer to the type and quantity of art glass used on pattern pieces (p41).

The quantities and types of materials listed are the minimum requirements for completing this project as illustrated, but materials may be substituted, if desired.

- A   12 in x 16 in opaque dark gray with white streaky (cut into 1⅞ in x 1⅞ in tesserae)
- B   4 in x 8 in opaque light gray with dark gray streaky (cut into 1⅞ in x 1⅞ in tesserae)
- C   4 in x 8 in opaque medium gray with white and pink streaky (cut into 1⅞ in x 1⅞ in tesserae)
- D   8 in x 12 in mirrored dark purple semi-antique (cut larger background piece; cut balance into ½ in x ½ in tesserae)
- E   7 in x 10 in translucent dark purple with blue and green streaky
- F   6 in x 7 in multi-color streaky full-antique
- G   6 in x 7 in translucent green, amber, and pink streaky
- H   6 in x 7 in emerald, chartreuse, and turquoise herringbone textured
- J   16 in x 23 in clear heavy-textured

NOTE   The letter I is not used in this listing.

Base/support structure

This window hanging consists of a translucent mosaic panel situated in the center of a wood base covered with glass tesserae. Follow basic guidelines given in Making Wood Base/Support Structures for Mosaic Panels and Wall Hangings (p28), taking note of these additional instructions:

1 Before fastening the wood trim moldings, an opening must be cut out of the center of the base piece (¾ in exterior grade plywood measuring 19½ in x 25⅝ in) to allow for installation of the translucent mosaic panel. Center a sheet of carbon paper and a copy of the pattern over the top surface of the base piece. Use a hard-tipped pen or pencil to trace pattern lines for the tesserae (A, B, C, D) to be applied to the base piece as well as the outline of the arched opening for the translucent mosaic panel. The tip and bottom of the arch are 2 in from the outside perimeter of the base piece.

2 Using a jigsaw, cut along the *inside* of the traced outline of the arch and remove plywood center from base piece.

3 On back side of base piece, use a router to make a ⅜ in rabbet (groove) along the edge of the arch cutout. This is where the translucent mosaic panel will be inserted.

4 Fasten cut lengths of wood trim molding around the perimeter of the wood base piece and fill any nail holes and gaps with wood filler. Use sandpaper to smooth away any rough edges along wood moldings and around arched opening.

5 Using cutout plywood piece as a template, trace outline of arch onto a sheet of graph paper. Measure and draw a second outline that is 5/16 in wide around the perimeter of the traced arch shape. With scissors or utility knife, cut out around the edge of this new outline to create a template from which you will cut out the two glass pieces that make up the base for the translucent mosaic panel.

6 Verify that the paper template fits within the recessed opening on the back side of the wood base. Make adjustments to template if necessary. The template must fit within the arch cutout and overlap onto the recessed edge by at least ¼ in.

7 Center pattern copy and a sheet of carbon paper over the paper template. Trace pattern outlines of the two base pieces (J, D) onto the template. Remove pattern copy and carbon paper and extend pattern

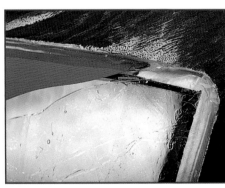

Note rabbet (groove) along the edge of the arch.

lines to the outside edge of the template. This gives an accurate guide for cutting glass pieces (J, D).

8 Cut (pp11, 14-16) clear heavy-textured glass piece (J) used for the base and mirrored dark purple semi-antique glass (D) for the background piece. Smooth (p19) away any rough edges along perimeter of both pieces.

9 Place wood base on work surface with back side facing upwards. Squeeze a slim bead of silicone into the corner of the recessed groove around the entire perimeter of arch opening. Place clear heavy-textured glass piece (J) into opening and press gently onto the silicone bead, *smooth side down*. Adhere mirrored piece (D) in the same manner, positioning piece with the silver backing facing *upwards* and glass side facing downwards. As indicated on pattern (p41), there is a narrow gap between these two pieces.

10 Allow silicone to set completely for approximately 24 hours before turning the base over. Use a utility knife or razor blade to remove any silicone that has oozed onto the front side of glass pieces (J, D).

11 Cover front surface of glass with masking tape, leaving an allowance of approximately ¼ in free of tape around perimeter of glass pieces.

Mosaic instructions

This mosaic panel is constructed using a combination of the Direct Method (p20) and the techniques described in Translucent Mosaics—Basic Steps (p26). Refer to the photograph of the finished mosaic as a guide for placement of the various types of tesserae.

1 Following instructions outlined for the Direct Method (p20), adhere the square tesserae (A, B, C), the strands of hair (E), and the rectangular mirrored pieces (D) onto the front surface of the wood portion of the base. Use a glass cutter or mosaic nippers to trim tesserae to fit within pattern lines. Mirrored tesserae (D) must not extend past the edge of the recessed opening where the glass base pieces are now firmly attached. Trim away shaded corner areas on the square tesserae (A, B, C) as indicated on the pattern. These spaces are to be filled with grout at a later stage.

2 Adhere ½ in x ½ in mirrored tesserae (D) to exposed wood edges between the arch framework that has already been tessellated and the glass base pieces. Allow tile adhesive to cure for approximately 24 hours.

3 Follow directions for Applying the Grout (p22) and Cleaning the Finished Piece (p23) to complete this portion of the mosaic. Use charcoal-tinted sanded grout to fill the interstices between the tesserae (A, B, C, D, E) situated on the wood portion of the base.

4 Remove the masking tape covering the two glass pieces that will serve as the base of the translucent mosaic section. Clean glass thoroughly to remove any trace of grout, adhesive, or grime.

5 Refer to instructions given for Translucent Mosaics (p26) to complete the mosaic. The translucent mosaic portion of this project is not grouted so the edges of each glass piece are left exposed. Edges can be smoothed (p19) with a diamond pad or wet/dry sandpaper. Whenever possible, glide each glass edge against a mirror grinding bit to achieve a more polished edge.

6 Refer to Mounting Wall Hangings, Plaques, and Mirrors (p29) for instructions about installing hanging hardware on the back of the base. Screw 2 cup hooks into a window frame. Use lengths of linked metal chain strong enough to bear the weight of the mosaic and suspend it in front of a window to illuminate the translucent portion of the piece.

NOTE   Using mirrored glass adds an interesting dimension to any mosaic project. Here are a few tips to keep in mind when working with larger pieces of mirror.

• Always cut mirror on the glass side, not the silvered underside.

• Small chips may appear in the silvering along the edge of a mirror if a piece requires grinding or shaping to fit the pattern. These chips may be visible once the mirror is in place and can mar the appearance of the mosaic. Chips can be removed or lessened by smoothing the silvered edge at a 45° angle using a glass grinder, wet/dry sandpaper, diamond pad, or carborundum stone. Refer to Smoothing Jagged and Sharp Edges on Mosaic Pieces (p19) for specific instructions about tools and techniques.

• To prevent discoloration or damage to the silver backing, use a neutral curing silicone, mirror mastic, or a non-corrosive tile adhesive to glue the mirrored pieces to the base/support structure.

• Cover the mirror surface with a single layer of overlapping rows of masking tape to prevent scratches while applying other tesserae and/or sanded grout.

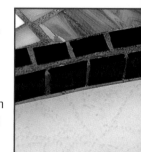

• Add depth to mosaic surface. Turn over some square tesserae (A, B, C) and apply them to the base with the reverse side up. Remember when transferring these shapes onto glass, turn over pattern before cutting the pieces out so they will fit within pattern outlines.

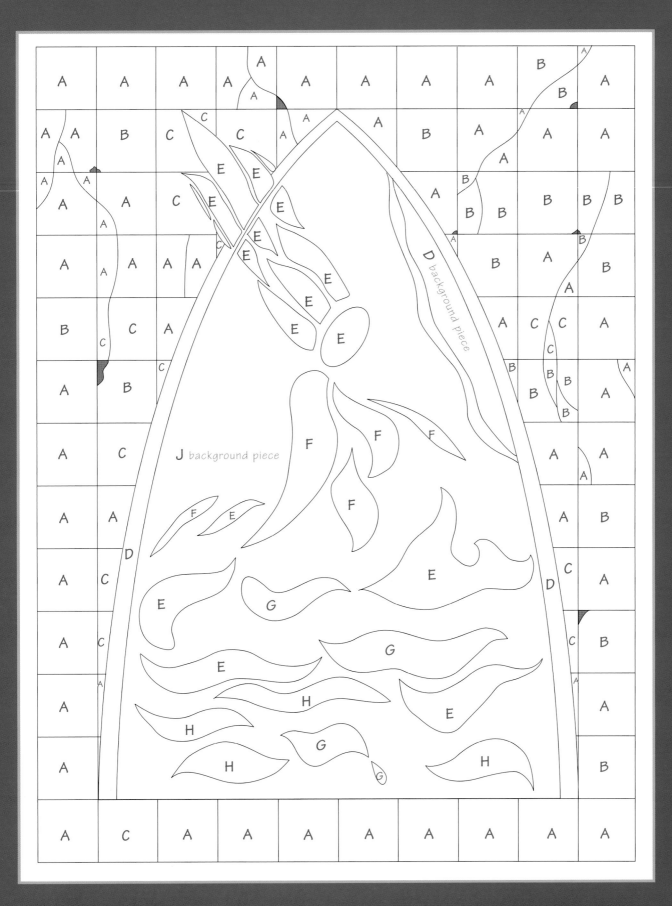

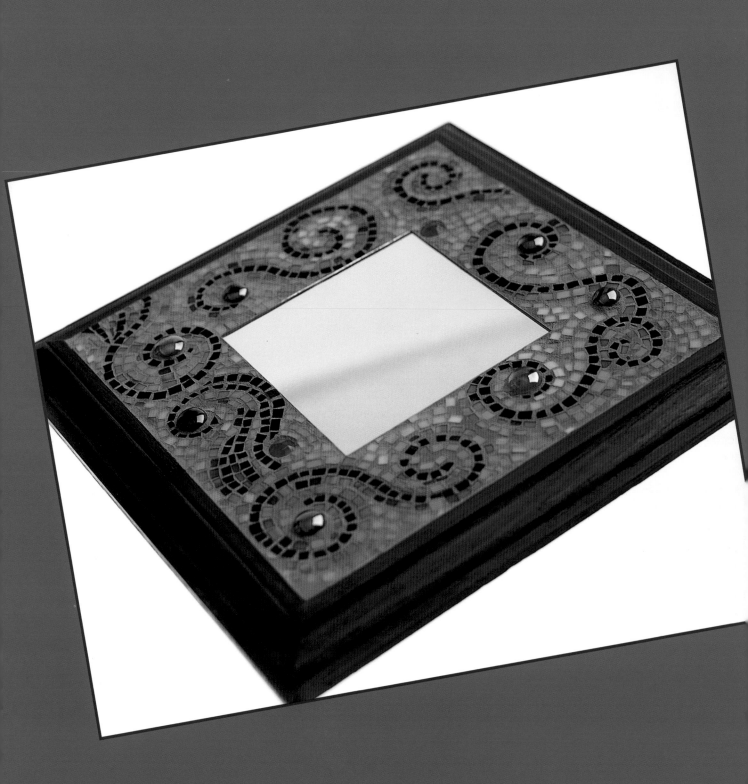

Whirlpool

wall mirror

Mosaic panel size   10 in square

Mosaic material required

Letters refer to the type and quantity of mosaic material used on pattern pieces (p44).

The quantities and types of materials listed are the minimum requirements for completing this project as illustrated, but materials may be substituted, if desired.

A   5 in x 5 in 3mm mirror

B   2–15mm blue round faceted glass jewels

C   2 iridescent lilac glass nuggets (medium size)

D   5 iridescent black glass nuggets (medium size)

E   4 in x 5 in translucent dark purple art glass (cut into $\frac{1}{4}$ in x $\frac{1}{4}$ in tesserae)

F   4 in x 5 in opaque steel blue with white wisps art glass (cut into $\frac{1}{4}$ in x $\frac{1}{4}$ in tesserae)

G   4 in x 5 in iridescent opaque gray with white wisps art glass (cut into $\frac{1}{4}$ in x $\frac{1}{4}$ in tesserae)

H   6 in x 6 in opaque pale purple with white wisps art glass (cut into $\frac{1}{4}$ in x $\frac{1}{4}$ in tesserae)

Base/support structure

Guidelines for constructing a base/support structure with wood trim molding are given in Making Wood Base/Support Structures for Mosaic Panels and Wall Hangings (p28).

Mosaic instructions

This wall mirror is constructed following instructions given for the Direct Method (p20) of mosaic construction. Refer to the photograph of the finished mosaic as a guide for placement of the various types of tesserae.

1   Adhere the mirror piece (A), jewels (B), and glass nuggets (C, D) to the base, as indicated on the project pattern, before gluing the rest of the tesserae in place.

2   Beginning with the innermost design line adjacent to a glass nugget that is the center of a swirl, apply tesserae (E, F, or G) one row at a time. Following the curvature of the pattern lines, work outward completing an entire swirl before beginning the next one. Use a glass cutter or mosaic nippers to trim tesserae to fit into spaces that are not large enough to accommodate an entire piece.

3   Using the opus vermiculatum method (p22) of mosaic application, complete the wall mirror by filling in the background with tesserae (H). These tesserae are adhered following the outlines of the swirls, row by row, until an area is filled.

4   Complete the mosaic by Applying the Grout (p22) and Cleaning the Finished Piece (p23). A pale mauve-tinted sanded grout is used to fill the interstices between the tesserae.

5   Refer to Mounting Wall Hangings, Plaques, and Mirrors (p29) for instructions on hanging the finished project.

NOTE   When working with larger pieces of mirrored glass

• Always cut mirror on the glass side, not the silvered underside.

• Small chips may appear in the silvering along the edge of a mirror if a piece requires grinding or shaping to fit the pattern. These chips can be visible once the mirror is in place and can mar the appearance of the mosaic. Chips can be removed or lessened by smoothing the silvered edge at a 45° angle using a glass grinder, wet/dry sandpaper, diamond pad, or carborundum stone. Refer to Smoothing Jagged and Sharp Edges on Mosaic Pieces (p19) section for specific instructions about tools and techniques.

• To prevent discoloration or damage to the silver backing, use a neutral curing silicone, mirror mastic, or a non-corrosive tile adhesive to glue the mirrored pieces to the base.

• Cover the mirror surface with a single layer of overlapping rows of masking tape to prevent scratches while applying other tesserae and/or sanded grout.

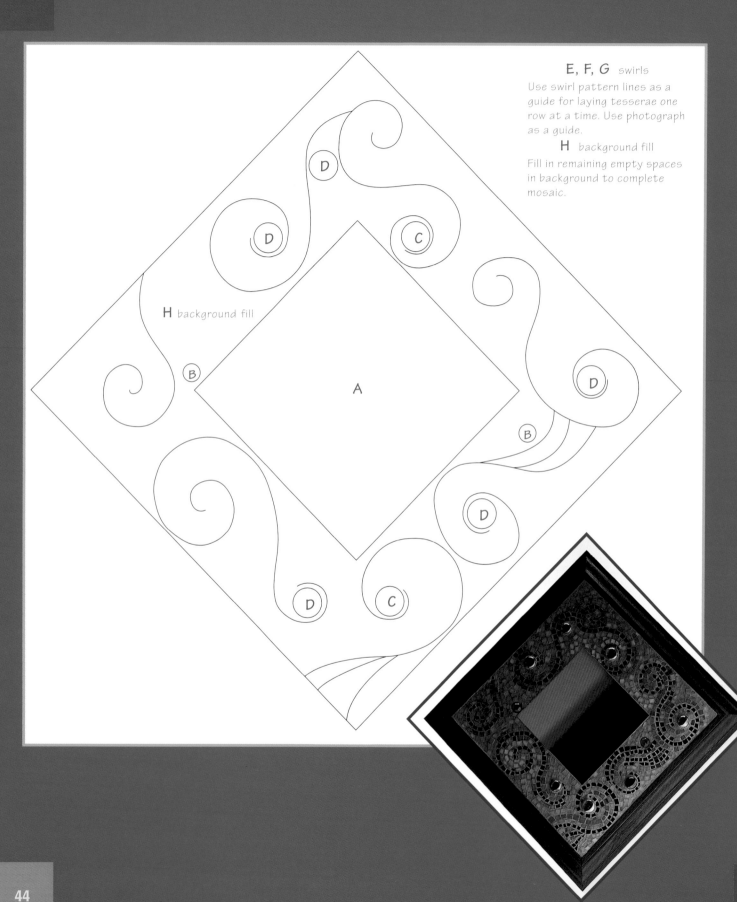

E, F, G swirls
Use swirl pattern lines as a
guide for laying tesserae one
row at a time. Use photograph
as a guide.

H background fill
Fill in remaining empty spaces
in background to complete
mosaic.

H background fill

D

D

C

B

A

D

B

D

D

C

44

Aristotle

small wall hanging

Mosaic panel size   10 in square

Mosaic material required

Letters refer to the type and quantity of mosaic material used on pattern pieces (p46).
The quantities and types of materials listed are the minimum requirements for completing this project as illustrated, but materials may be substituted, if desired.

A   92—¾ in x ¾ in translucent green and copper glass mosaic tiles
B   5 in x 8 in green with blue wisps art glass (cut into ⅜ in x ¼ in tesserae)
C   5 in x 8 in ivory with tan wisps art glass (cut into ⅜ in x ¼ in tesserae)
D   3 in x 3 in green ring mottle art glass
E   4 in x 6 in brown with tan and white wisps art glass (cut turtle's larger back pieces; cut balance into ¼ in x ¼ in tesserae)

Base/support structure

1 piece 10 in x 10 in—¾ in exterior grade plywood

Mosaic instructions

This mosaic panel can be fabricated using either the Direct Method (p20) or the Indirect Method (p23) of mosaic construction. Choose the method you prefer. Refer to the photograph of the finished mosaic as a guide for placement of the various types of tesserae.

1   Begin by adhering the glass mosaic tiles (A) that form the border around the mosaic pattern. Space tiles evenly, approximately ¹⁄₁₆ in apart. Do not extend over the edge of the base.

2   Proceed to cement the mosaic pieces that form the turtle (D, E) and the small section of water (B) in the top left corner of the pattern. The larger spaces between the individual tessera of the turtle are filled in with grout to emphasize his shell.

3   Outline the turtle's rounded body shape with a row of tesserae that represents the sandbar (C).

4   Use the wave-like pattern line that separates the sandbar (C) from the larger body of water (B) as a guide to fill in the remaining areas. Changing the adamanto (flow) of the tesserae will create the look of rippling waves of water lapping along the edges of the sandbar. To break up the expanse of water (B), place a couple of sand (C) tesserae amongst the waves.

5   Lay the base flat on the work surface and adhere glass mosaic tiles (A) along the outside edge of the plywood. Each of the four sides will require 12 tiles evenly spaced approximately ¹⁄₁₆ in apart. Allow the adhesive to set for approximately 24 hours.

6   Complete the mosaic following instructions for Applying the Grout (p22) and Cleaning the Finished Piece (p23). A soft sea green-tinted non-sanded grout is used to fill the interstices between the tesserae.

7   Refer to Mounting Wall Hangings, Plaques, and Mirrors (p29) or instructions on hanging the finished mosaic.

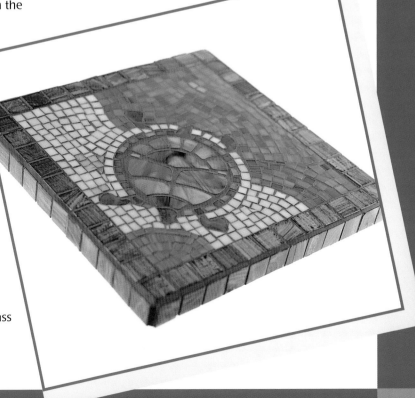

C background fill

B background fill

B
background
fill

Night & Day

bed tray

Mosaic panel size   18 in wide by 12 in high

Mosaic material required

Letters refer to the type and quantity of art glass used on pattern pieces (p50).

The quantities and types of materials listed are the minimum requirements for completing this project as illustrated, but materials may be substituted, if desired.

A   3 in x 6 in opaque white with cranberry pink and blue streaks
B   2 in x 4 in black
C   6 in x 9 in iridescent opaque white (cut phases of moon; and balance into ½ in x ½ in tesserae)
D   4 in x 4 in mirrored dark blue semi-antique (cut 68—$^3/_8$ in X $^3/_8$ in tesserae; cut eye pieces from balance)
E   1 in x 2 in mirrored light blue semi-antique
F   6 in x 8 in mirrored dark amber semi-antique (cut sun face pieces; and balance into small random-size tesserae)
G   5 in x 6 in mirrored light amber semi-antique (cut into small random-size tesserae)
H   4 in x 5 in iridescent red with white wispy (cut sun mouth pieces; and balance into small random-size tesserae)
J   2 in x 2 in opaque pink with white wisps
K   2 in x 4 in 3mm mirror
L   6 in x 8 in mixed blues ring mottle (cut into ½ in x ½ in tesserae)
M   4 in x 6 in opaque white with blue and purple streaks (cut into ½ in x ½ in tesserae)
N   8 in x 12 in mixed purples opal (cut into ½ in x ½ in tesserae)

NOTE The letter I is not used in this listing.

Base/support structure

Wood tray

4—8 in decorative wood legs (optional)

2 large serving utensils (optional)

8 assorted amber and red glass nuggets (optional)

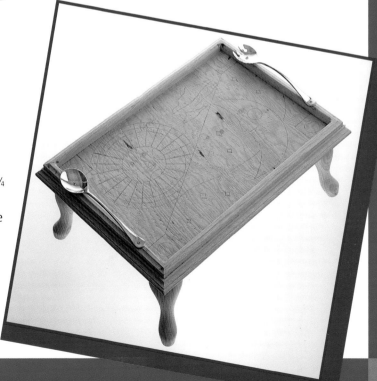

1   Use a pre-fabricated wood tray for the base or make your own.

2   Refer to guidelines for constructing a wall hanging base/support structure as described on p28. The mosaic panel is 18 in wide x 12 in high. Cut an 18 ½ in x 12½ in ¾ in exterior grade plywood base piece creating an ¼ in allowance on each side to accommodate placement of the mosaic panel.

3   To prevent dishware and utensils from sliding off the tray, use a wide enough wood trim molding along the tray perimeter to produce a raised edge approximately 1 in high.

4   Fasten an 8-in wood furniture leg to the underside of four corners of tray.

5 To make the handles, use a power drill to put holes through either end of 2 large and sturdy serving utensils. Carefully bend the utensils to create a curve large enough to accommodate a hand grasping the tray handles.

6 Pre-drill holes in the wood trim molding at each end of the tray. Align the utensils along the top of the molding and use a pencil to mark the location where the holes should be drilled.

7 Attach utensils to tray with No. 6 wood screws, 1 in long.

8 Use silicone or epoxy to glue glass nuggets over the tops of the screws, adding a design element that camouflages the screw heads.

9 Alternatively, attach 2 ready-made handles to the tray.

Mosaic instructions

Fabricate the mosaic panel by following instructions given for Indirect (Reverse) Method (p23). Refer to the photograph of the finished mosaic for placement of the various types of tesserae. The shaped glass pieces that comprise the most prominent design features of the mosaic should be placed on the clear adhesive-backed vinyl first.

1 Place these cut glass pieces onto the vinyl before filling the remainder of the mosaic with the various background tesserae: clouds (A); four corners representing phases of the moon (B, C, D); eyes of sun and man-in-the-moon (D, E); sun cheeks (F), chin (F) and mouth (H); man-in-the-moon cheek (J); and stars (K).

2 Highlight the sun nose by applying small pieces of tesserae (F) along the pattern lines outlining its shape.

3 Fill in the remainder of sun face and rays with random-size tesserae (F, G, H), as marked on the pattern. Start at the center of the face and work your way outward until completely filled in.

4 Complete the man-in-the-moon by using the opus vermiculatum method (p22) to apply the tesserae (C). Begin by applying a perimeter row of tesserae (C) within the pattern outline. Using a glass cutter or mosaic nippers, trim tesserae to fit into spaces that are not large enough to accommodate a whole piece. When the entire row around the perimeter has been completed, start a new row inside the one just completed. Using this method, fill in the remainder of the moon.

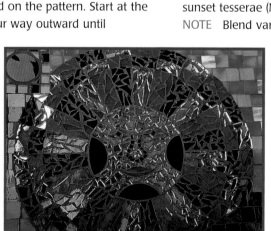

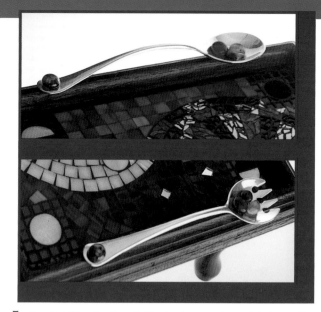

5 Begin filling in the night sky by starting with the Milky Way located in the lower portion of the mosaic. Align a row of tesserae (N) along the underside of the curving design line that separates the Milky Way from the rest of the mosaic. The line acts as a guide for the adamanto (flow) of the tesserae, resulting in undulating rows that suggest movement. Use paler shades of purple tesserae (N) and randomly intermingle several lighter tesserae (M) to achieve the Milky Way look.

6 Continue by filling in the upper portion of the night sky using the opus tesselatum method (p22) to apply the tesserae. Use darker shades of purple tesserae (N) adding in a few random pieces of blue daytime tesserae (L) and lighter sunset tesserae (M).

NOTE   Blend various tesserae (L, M, N) along the diagonal pattern line to create a pleasing transition from daylight to nighttime.

7 Apply daytime sky tesserae (L) to the vinyl. Intermingle several purple tesserae (N) and place a number of lighter sunset tesserae (M) around the cloud pieces (A).

8 After centering and adhering the mosaic to the base, use random-size tesserae (F) to fill any empty space between the mosaic panel and the tray wood trim.

9 Complete the mosaic by following instructions given for Applying the Grout (p22) and Cleaning the Finished Piece (p23). A charcoal-tinted non-sanded grout is used to fill interstices between tesserae.

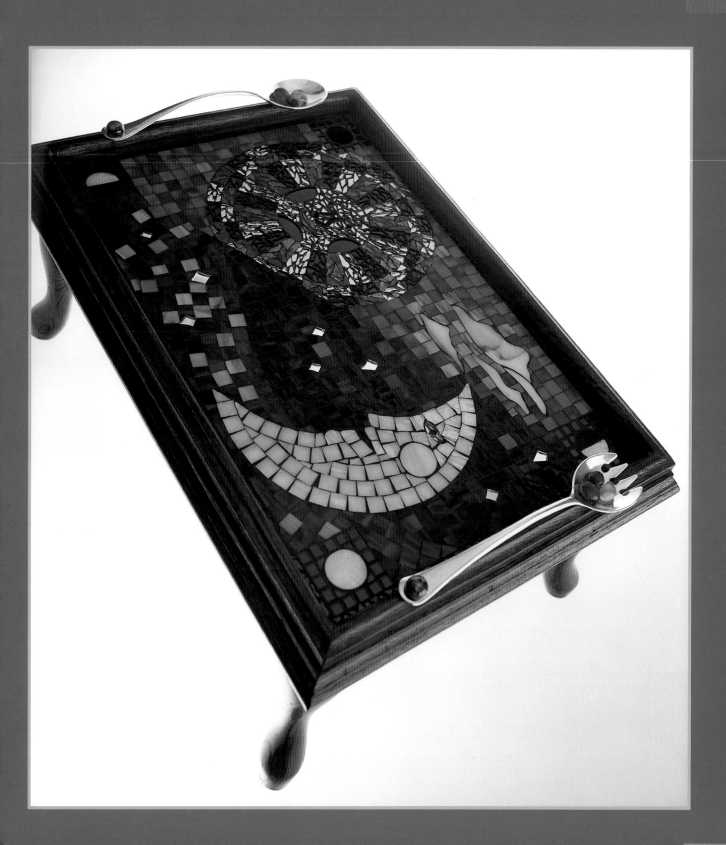

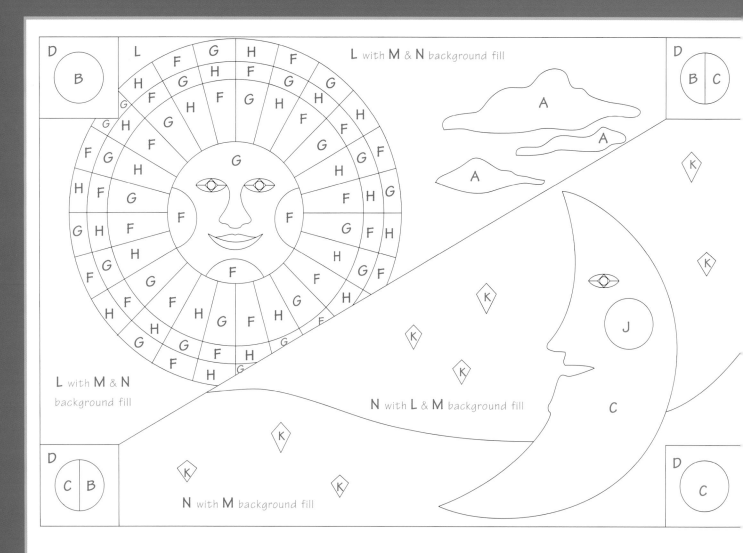

L with M & N background fill

L with M & N background fill

N with L & M background fill

N with M background fill

D moon eye center piece
E moon other eye pieces

D sun eye center piece
E sun other eye pieces
H sun lip pieces
F sun nose outline pieces

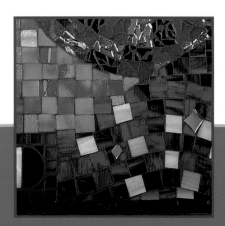

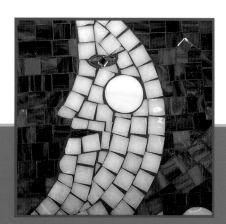

Night Moves

small wall hanging

Mosaic panel size   **10 in square**

Mosaic material required

Letters refer to the type and quantity of mosaic material used on pattern pieces (p52).
The quantities and types of materials listed are the minimum requirements for completing this
project as illustrated, but materials may be substituted, if desired.

A   1–12 in x 12 in sheet of 1 in unglazed commercial granite mosaic tiles
B   4 in x 8 in black art glass
C   5 in x 10 in iridescent black art glass
D   4 in x 5 in opaque red art glass
E   2 in x 5 in iridescent opaque red art glass
F   2 iridescent black glass nuggets (medium size)
G   15mm red round faceted glass jewel

Base/support structure

Guidelines for constructing a base with wood trim molding
are given in Making Wood Base/Support Structures for
Mosaic Panels and Wall Hangings (p28).

Mosaic instructions

Fabricate mosaic panel following
instructions given for the Direct Method
(p20). Refer to the photograph of the
finished mosaic as a guide for placement
of the various types of tesserae.

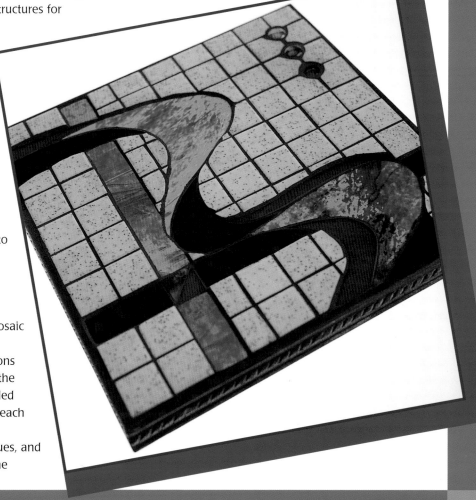

1   Adhere cut glass shapes (B, C, D, E),
glass nuggets (F), and faceted glass jewel
(G) to the base.

2   Fill in background with mosaic tiles (A).
Apply them using opus tesselatum method
(p22). Use glass or tile nippers to trim tiles to
fit into spaces that are not large enough to
accommodate a whole tile.

3   Apply a tile sealer to the surface of
unglazed tiles (A) before grouting. Colored
grout may stain or tint porous unglazed mosaic
tiles if surfaces are not protected.

4   Complete mosaic by following instructions
for Applying the Grout (p22) and Cleaning the
Finished Piece (p23). A charcoal-tinted sanded
grout is used to fill the interstices between each
tessera.

5   Refer to Mounting Wall Hangings, Plaques, and
Mirrors (p29) for instructions on hanging the
finished mosaic.

• Commercial mosaic tiles often come attached on a net or paper backing in sheets of approximately 1 sq ft, depending on the size of the individual tiles. The sheet can be adhered to a base in one piece or tiles can be easily removed from the backing as needed. For this project, tiles are pulled from the backing and individually trimmed and adhered to the base with ceramic tile adhesive.

• Add depth to the mosaic surface by turning over the curved black art glass pieces (B) and applying them to the base with the reverse side up. The underside of many art glass sheets is slightly textured creating a contrast with the smoother topside. Remember to turn over the pattern when transferring these shapes onto the glass sheet before cutting them so that they will fit within the pattern outlines.

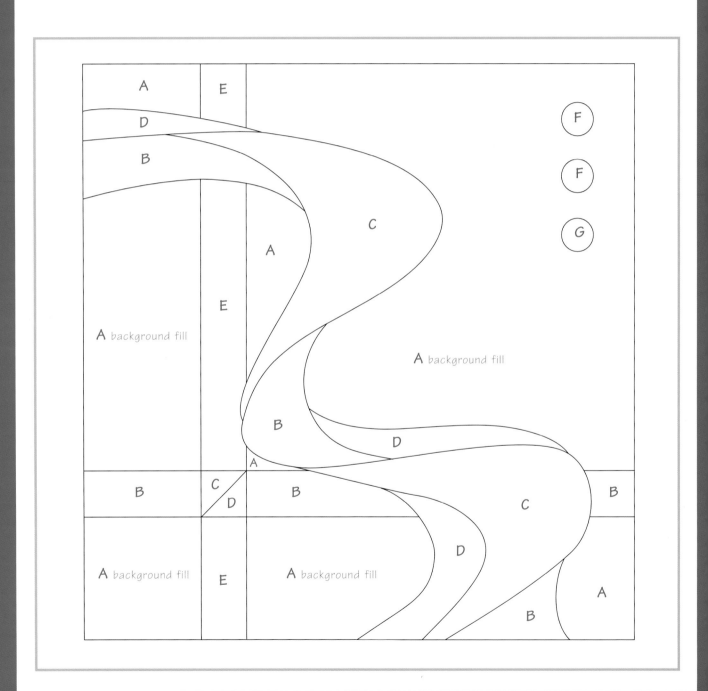

Hearts • Leaves

translucent window hangings

Mosaic panel size	Hearts #1 and #2	6¼ in wide by 10 in high
	Large Leaf	6¼ in wide by 10½ in high
	Small Leaf	2¾ in wide by 4 in high

Mosaic material required

Letters refer to the type and quantity of art glass used on pattern pieces (p56).
The quantities and types of materials listed are the minimum requirements for completing this project as illustrated, but materials may be substituted, if desired.

A   translucent iridescent red with white wisps (cut into random-size tesserae)
B   iridescent clear textured (cut into random-size tesserae)
C   translucent amber crushed glass frit
D   translucent red crushed glass frit
E   translucent spring green with white, blue and pink streaks (cut into random-size tesserae)
F   translucent dark green crushed glass frit

for each large leaf and hearts #1 and #2—6 in x 6 in of glass tesserae
for each small leaf—2 in x 3 in of glass tesserae

Base/support structure

Heart #1   7 in x 10 in clear glue chip art glass
Heart #2   7 in x 10 in clear 4mm leaf patterned architectural glass
Large Leaf   7 in x 10 in clear 4mm leaf patterned architectural glass
Small Leaf   3 in x 4 in clear 4mm leaf patterned architectural glass
16-gauge brass wire
Assorted crystals and glass beads (optional)
Heavyweight monofilament (fishing) line

The bases for these translucent mosaic hangings are made with clear textured glass and brass wire. Refer to Preparing the Base/Support Structure (p27) for general information before beginning this project.

1   Trace (p10) the outline of the chosen heart or leaf project onto the required piece of clear textured glass. Using a glass cutter, cut (p11) and break (p14) the shape of the base away from the sheet of glass.

2   Smooth (p19) jagged edges where necessary. If possible, use a mirror grinding bit to achieve a more polished edge.

3   Brass wire is adhered to the base as a decorative accent as well as a hanging device. Use needlenose pliers to bend lengths of brass wire to conform to the dotted lines drawn on the project pattern. Trim excess wire with wire cutters.

4   Place the base *textured side down* onto the pattern and apply slim beads of silicone to the glass surface in several locations along the dotted pattern lines. Lay the bent wire flat against the top side of the base and onto the beads of silicone. With a palette knife or craft stick, remove excessive amounts of silicone on either side of the wire.

5   Secure wire to the base by taping the wire to the glass at the locations that are free of silicone. Allow silicone to set for approximately 24 hours before removing tape and adhering tesserae and glass frit to the base.

Mosaic instructions

These translucent window hangings are constructed following instructions given for Adhering the Mosaic Pieces to the Base/Support Structure (p27). Refer to the photograph of the finished mosaic as a guide for placement of the various types of tesserae.

1   Apply a thin layer of silicone, one section at a time, to the base and fill in each area with the required random-size tesserae. Leave a space of approximately ¹⁄₁₆ in wide between the tesserae and about ¹⁄₁₆ in from the outside edge of the base.

2   To maintain transparency, these translucent hangings are not grouted. Crushed glass frit is used to fill the interstices between the tesserae and as a distinctive decorative component. Sprinkle glass frit over each section as it is completed, using a palette knife or craft stick to press frit into the silicone that is present between the tesserae. Turn the base over and suspend above a container. Gently tap base to allow excess frit to fall into the container. The frit can then be used for another section or project.

3 Spread silicone over the brass wire running down the center of the base and in any remaining open areas. Use a small brush to apply silicone in narrow spaces.

4 Distribute a generous amount of specified glass frit onto the siliconed areas, pressing frit into the silicone as described in step 2.

5 After 72 hours, a protective clear coat can be sprayed over the surface of the hanging to keep any exposed areas of brass from tarnishing and to act as additional fixative for the glass frit. Follow manufacturer's directions carefully.

6 Assorted crystals and glass beads can be attached to the brass wire to complement the finished hanging.

7 Screw a cup hook into a window frame and suspend the hanging from a length of heavyweight monofilament (fishing) line or a fine-linked metal chain strong enough to bear the weight of the hanging.

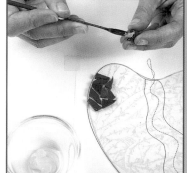
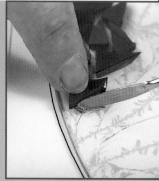
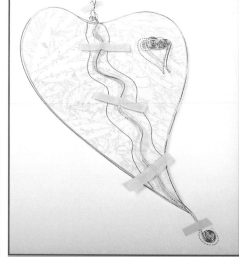

NOTE

• Glass frits are made by several art glass manufacturers and are generally used for glass fusing, casting, and blowing. Frits can be purchased at many stained glass studios. Make your own glass frits by crushing and grinding pieces of glass into small fragments.

1 Wrap pieces of glass in heavy fabric or several layers of newspaper and hit with a hammer until glass is crushed to the desired size.

2 Place several smaller pieces of glass into a heavy-duty metal mortar or bucket and grind glass into frit with a pestle or hammer head.

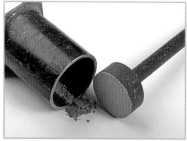

• When using monofilament line to suspend a mosaic hanging, check the line periodically and replace as necessary. Exposure to sun UV rays can damage or cause the line to disintegrate over time.

• Suction cups are not recommended for hanging mosaics due to the weight of the mosaic. As well, the cups dry out and may detach from the window glass.

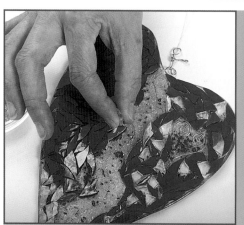
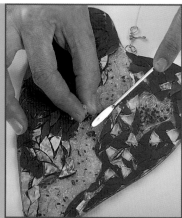

Safety reminder Always wear safety glasses or goggles and a work apron. When using silicone and other adhesives that give off vapors, work in a well-ventilated area and wear a respirator (if necessary). To avoid inhaling airborne glass dust and particles, always wear a respirator or dust mask when crushing glass into small fragments. Individuals sensitive to chemicals should wear rubber or latex gloves to avoid skin contact and safety goggles to protect eyes from vapors.

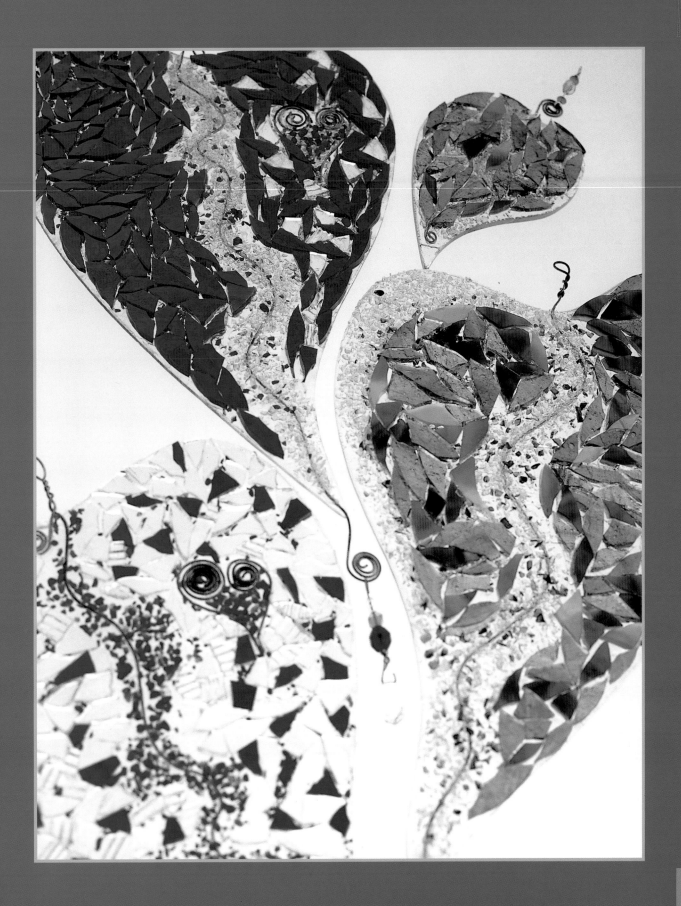

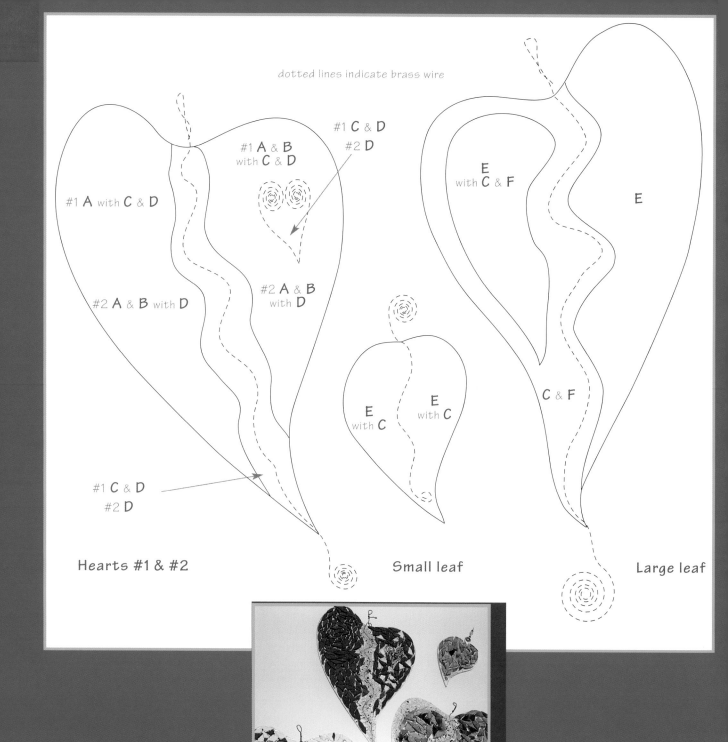

dotted lines indicate brass wire

#1 **C** & **D**
#2 **D**

#1 **A** & **B**
with **C** & **D**

#1 **A** with **C** & **D**

E
with **C** & **F**

E

#2 **A** & **B** with **D**

#2 **A** & **B**
with **D**

E
with **C**

E
with **C**

C & **F**

#1 **C** & **D**
#2 **D**

Hearts #1 & #2

Small leaf

Large leaf

Summer Vines

small wall hanging

Mosaic panel size   10 in square

Mosaic material required

Letters refer to the type and quantity of mosaic material used on pattern pieces (p58).
The quantities and types of materials listed are the minimum requirements for completing this project as illustrated, but materials may be substituted, if desired.

A   4—¾ in x ¾ in translucent copper glass mosaic tiles
B   88—¾ in x ¾ in translucent pink and copper glass mosaic tiles
C   6 in x 6 in opaque medium and dark green art glass (cut into small random-size tesserae)
D   2 in x 6 in opaque brown art glass (cut into small random-size tesserae)
E   4 in x 8 in opaque white with cranberry pink and blue streaky art glass (cut into medium random-size tesserae)

Base/support structure

1 piece 10 in x 10 in—¾ in exterior grade plywood

Mosaic instructions

This mosaic panel can be fabricated using either the Direct Method (p20) or the Indirect Method (p23) of mosaic construction. Choose the method you prefer. Refer to the photograph of the finished mosaic as a guide for placement of the various types of tesserae.

1   Adhere vine tesserae (D), placing pieces within the pattern lines. Proceed by applying rows of random-size green tesserae (C), outlining each leaf shape and the center vein. Use random method to fill remaining inner portion of each leaf with green tesserae.

2   Adhere glass mosaic tiles (A, B) that form the border around mosaic pattern. Space tiles evenly, approximately ¹⁄₁₆ in apart. Do not extend over edge of pattern. Use a glass cutter or mosaic nippers to trim tiles (B) that do not fit in spaces.

3   Fill the mosaic background with random-size tesserae (E). Start in the center and work outward until the background is completely filled in.

4   Before grouting mosaic panel, finish outside edges of the base. Lay base flat on work surface and adhere glass mosaic tiles (B) along outside edge of plywood. Each of the four sides will require 12 tiles evenly spaced, approximately ¹⁄₁₆ in apart. Allow adhesive to set for approximately 24 hours.

5   Complete mosaic piece by following instructions for

Applying the Grout (p22) and Cleaning the Finished Piece (p23). An ivory-tinted sanded grout is used to fill interstices between tesserae.

6   Refer to Mounting Wall Hangings, Plaques, and Mirrors (p29) for instructions on hanging the finished piece.

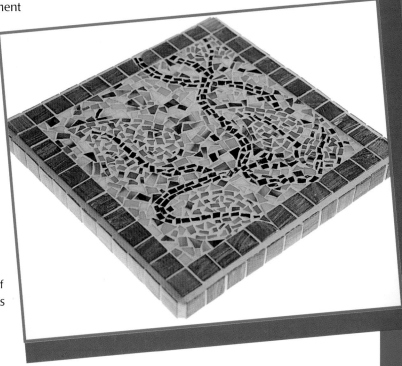

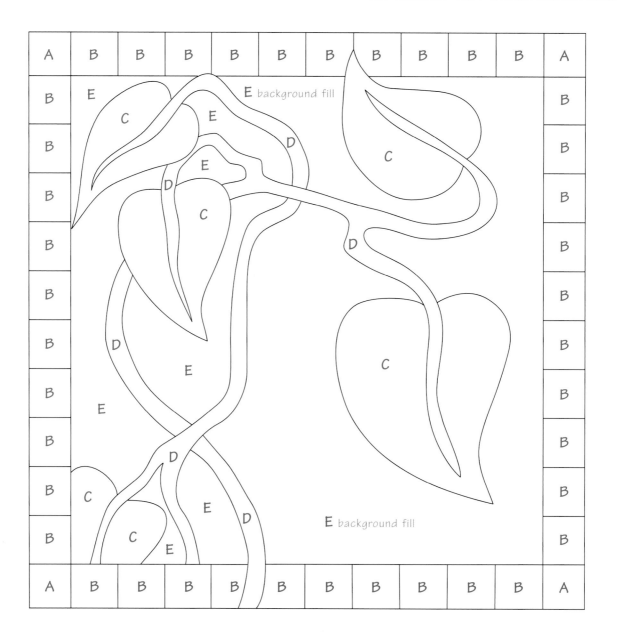

Swirl

lamp shade

Mosaic material required

Approximately ½ sq ft of assorted translucent and opalescent art glasses are needed to cover this glass shade—5 in tall with a bottom diameter measuring 4⅛ in and a top diameter of 2 in. The quantities and types of art glass used will vary depending on the size of shade, availability of materials, and personal color preferences. Cut the art glasses into tesserae of random sizes and shapes no more than ⅜ in x ⅜ in.

Base/support structure

The glass shade is used as a base for this translucent mosaic project. The lamp shade and electrical fixture are of the ready-made commercial variety available in home decorating stores. The shade is made of clear glass with a painted white interior that hides the electrical components and softens the glare of the light bulb.

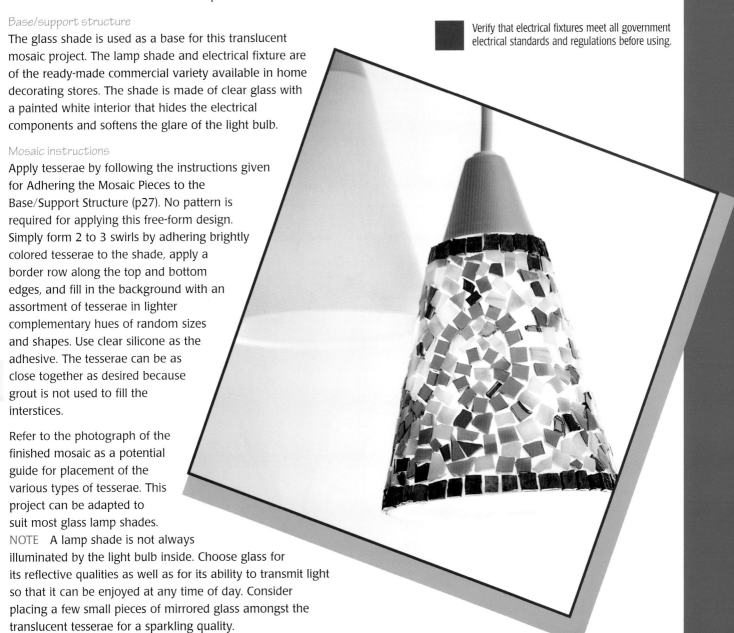

Verify that electrical fixtures meet all government electrical standards and regulations before using.

Mosaic instructions

Apply tesserae by following the instructions given for Adhering the Mosaic Pieces to the Base/Support Structure (p27). No pattern is required for applying this free-form design. Simply form 2 to 3 swirls by adhering brightly colored tesserae to the shade, apply a border row along the top and bottom edges, and fill in the background with an assortment of tesserae in lighter complementary hues of random sizes and shapes. Use clear silicone as the adhesive. The tesserae can be as close together as desired because grout is not used to fill the interstices.

Refer to the photograph of the finished mosaic as a potential guide for placement of the various types of tesserae. This project can be adapted to suit most glass lamp shades.

NOTE   A lamp shade is not always illuminated by the light bulb inside. Choose glass for its reflective qualities as well as for its ability to transmit light so that it can be enjoyed at any time of day. Consider placing a few small pieces of mirrored glass amongst the translucent tesserae for a sparkling quality.

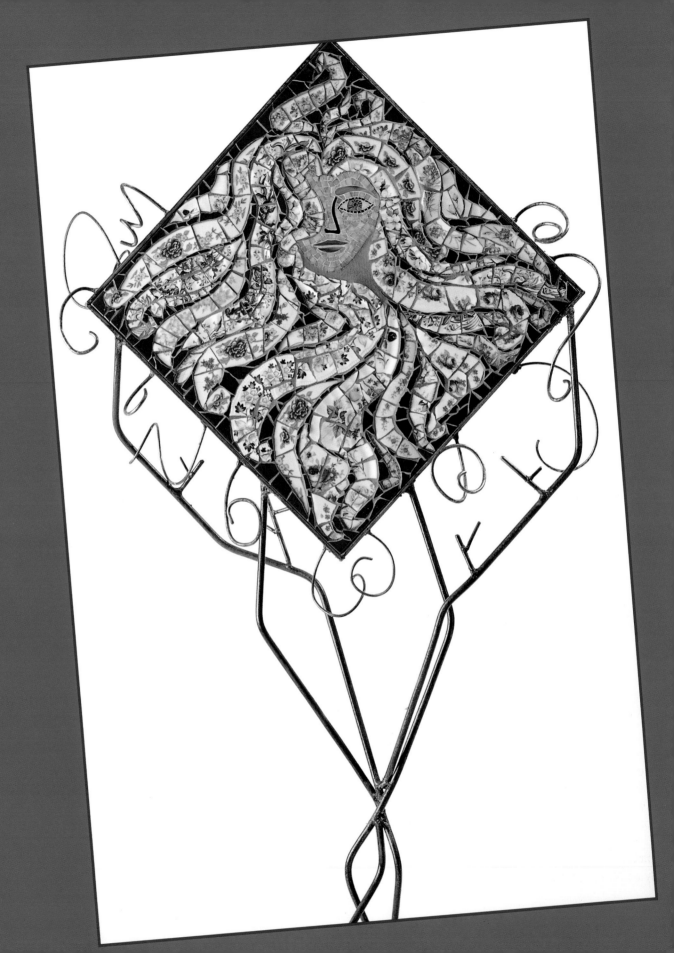

Arrival of Spring

mosaic panel

Mosaic panel size   **18 in square**

Mosaic material required

Letters refer to the type and quantity of mosaic material used on pattern pieces (p63).
The quantities and types of materials listed are the minimum requirements for completing this project as illustrated, but materials may be substituted, if desired.

A   4 in x 4 in opaque iridescent peach with white wisps art glass (cut into tesserae approximately $\frac{1}{4}$ in x $\frac{1}{4}$ in)

B   1 in x 3 in opaque spring green with white wisps art glass

C   2 in x 3 in translucent dark brown art glass

D   1 in x 2 in opaque cranberry pink with white wisps art glass

E   1 in x 1 in black art glass (cut into tesserae approximately $\frac{1}{8}$ in wide)

F   1 in x 1 in opaque iridescent white art glass

G   1 in x 1 in green dichroic glass

H   1 in x 1 in blue dichroic glass

J   15 to 20 assorted china and ceramic floral patterned plates

K   4–4 in x 4 in forest green glazed ceramic wall tiles (thin)

NOTE   The letter I was not used in this listing.

Base/support structure

This mosaic panel is constructed on an 18 in x 18 in piece of $\frac{3}{4}$ in exterior grade plywood. The finished mosaic is inserted into a custom designed metal frame and stand affixed to a revolving pedestal. An 18 in x 18 in piece of 3mm mirror is adhered with neutral curing silicone to the exposed plywood on the reverse side of the mosaic. Several translucent glass leaves are glued to the mirror in a random fashion to complete the piece.

If you do not have the tools or skills to construct the base/support structure as illustrated in the photograph, create a wall hanging. Follow guidelines for constructing a base/support structure with wood trim molding given in Making Wood Base/Support Structures for Mosaic Panels and Wall Hangings (p28).

Mosaic instructions

This mosaic panel is constructed using a combination of the Indirect Method (p23) and the Direct Method (p20) of mosaic construction. Use the indirect method to form the many small tesserae into the delicate features of Spring's face. The assorted china and ceramic plates (J) that are broken into the tesserae that make up Spring's strands of hair are varied in pattern, size, and thickness, making the direct method the only feasible way to adhere these pieces to the base. Apply ceramic tile in the mosaic background directly to the base to fill in the larger spaces between and around the various tesserae. Refer to the photograph of the finished mosaic as a guide for placement of the various types of tesserae.

1 Using instructions given for the Indirect Method (p23), position glass pieces that form the features of Spring's face onto the adhesive-backed vinyl first: eyebrow (B), nose (C), mouth (D), eye (E, F, G, H). The outline of the nose has been cut using a glass band saw. If you do not have access to a band saw, cut tesserae approximately $\frac{1}{4}$ in wide and use pattern outline of the nose as a guide for placement.

2 Complete Spring's face by filling in with tesserae (A) row by row, in the opus vermiculatum (p22) style. Follow the outline of the face and each of the facial features, working inward until the face is completely filled. Using a glass cutter or mosaic nippers, trim tesserae to fit into spaces that do not accommodate a whole piece.

3 Use a utility knife to trim away excess vinyl around the outline of the face.

4 Spread a thin layer of ceramic tile adhesive onto the base, staying within pattern outline of the face. Align the tesserae-laden vinyl over the pattern outline traced onto the base and lay the mosaic onto the adhesive, pressing gently into place. Leaving the vinyl in place, allow the adhesive to set completely for at least 24 hours.

5   Cut (pp18-19) and break the assorted china and ceramic plates into smaller tesserae that will fit within the outlines of Spring's strands of hair. Here are a few tips to keep in mind when using china and ceramic dinnerware to make tesserae for this project:

• For easier cutting and shaping, choose dinnerware with floral patterns on the flattest areas of the plates.

• To differentiate the strands from one another, use one particular floral pattern and/or color throughout the outline of each strand.

• Use plate rims to accentuate the curvaceousness of the strands by positioning the rounded edges along the perimeter of the pattern outlines.

6   Where necessary, smooth jagged edges (p19) with a carborundum stone, wet/dry sandpaper, or diamond pad, or by grozing (p19) with pliers.

7   Following instructions for Adhering the Mosaic Pieces to the Base/Support Structure (p21), affix tesserae directly to the base filling in one strand at a time. Buttering (p22) the back of a tessera with additional adhesive may be required to fill small spaces created if a tessera does not fit flush with surface of the base.

8   Cut, shape (p18), and glue pieces of green ceramic tile (K) to the base to fill in the larger spaces between the strands of hair and around the perimeter of the mosaic pattern. If the base is not framed by wood trim molding, leave an allowance of $\frac{1}{16}$ in between the edge of the tesserae and the edge of the base to accommodate a border row of tesserae or a frame, as shown in the photograph (p60). Align rounded outermost edges of the tile pieces along the perimeter of the mosaic to attain a more refined appearance. Once the background is completely filled with tesserae, allow adhesive to cure for at least 24 hours.

9   Complete the mosaic by Applying the Grout (p22) and Cleaning the Finished Piece (p23). This mosaic is grouted with two distinctive colors of sanded grout. Before peeling the adhesive-backed vinyl from the surface of Spring's face, use a leaf green-tinted grout to fill the interstices between the strands of hair, around the perimeter of the mosaic, and in the open area below the face. *See* Note (p85) about grouting large open areas. When the grout has cured and is completely dry, remove adhesive-backed vinyl from the face area. Use a utility knife or dental pick to remove any green grout between the face tesserae. Then apply an ivory-tinted grout filling in only the interstices between the tesserae that comprise Spring's face. Gently wipe or scrape away any ivory-tinted grout beyond the outline of the face and allow

the grout to set.

10   If you created a wall hanging, refer to Mounting Wall Hangings, Plaques, and Mirrors (p29) for instructions on hanging the finished mosaic.

NOTE

• When making small tesserae, use tile or glass mosaic cutters (nippers) to divide a larger tessera in half and from there into smaller shapes and sizes.

• Garage sales, thrift shops, and flea markets are a great and inexpensive source for china and ceramic dinnerware and various objects for base/support structures.

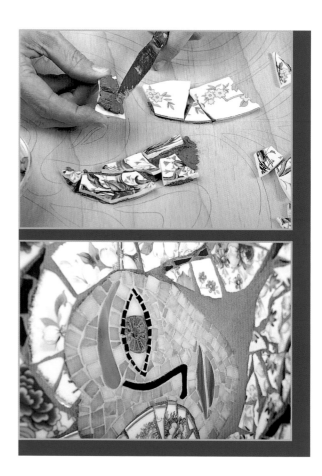

Safety reminder   Always wear safety glasses or goggles when using any glass or tile cutting and/or breaking tool.

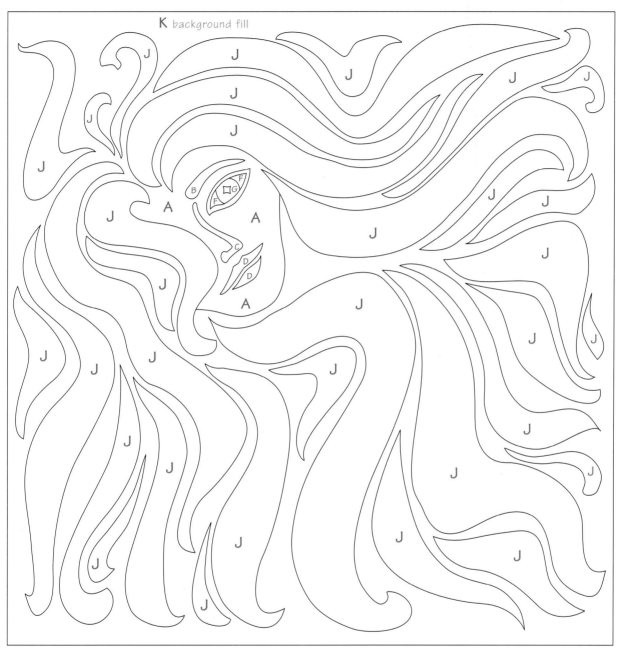

K background fill

A face   E eye outline   J hair
B eyebrow   F white of eye   K background fill
C nose   G iris
D mouth   H pupil

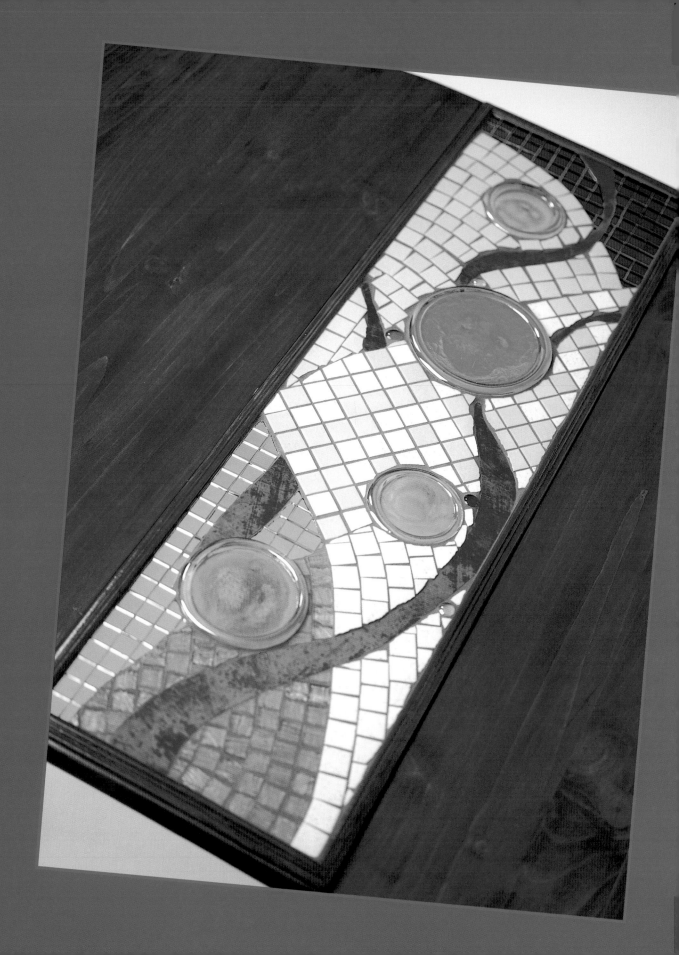

Just Visiting

Mosaic panel size   10½ in wide by 40 in long

Mosaic material required

Letters refer to the type and quantity of mosaic material used on pattern pieces (p66).
The quantities and types of materials listed are the minimum requirements for completing this project as illustrated, but materials may be substituted, if desired.

A	2 small (3 in to 4 in) round translucent iridescent amber pressed glass coasters
B	1 medium (4 in to 5 in) round translucent iridescent amber pressed glass coaster
C	1 large (6 in to 7 in) round translucent iridescent green pressed glass coaster
D	2 iridescent amber glass nuggets (medium size)
E	1 amber glass nugget (medium size)
F	1 red glass nugget (medium size)
G	12 in x 14 in translucent iridescent red art glass
H	50 to 55—¾ in x ¾ in translucent copper glass mosaic tiles
J	6 in x 8 in mirrored light green semi-antique art glass (cut into ¾ in x ¾ in tesserae)
K	6 in x 10 in mirrored dark green semi-antique art glass (cut into ¾ in x ¾ in tesserae)

3 to 4—12 in x 12 in sheets of 1 in x 1 in unglazed commercial tan and beige with tan mix mosaic tiles

L	tan and beige with tan mix
M	beige with tan
N	tan

NOTE the letter I is not used in this listing.

Base/support structure

Use the leaf from a wood dining table as the base for this mosaic.

1 Prepare the wood surface by removing any lacquers, paints, or sealants, and abrade with sandpaper.

2 Create a framework for the mosaic by fastening ¾ in wood trim molding along the top edges of the table leaf and stain or paint to match the tabletop. Refer to Making Wood Base/Support Structures for Mosaic Panels and Wall Hangings (p28).

Mosaic instructions

The mosaic panel for this project is constructed following instructions given for the Direct Method (p20). Refer to the photograph of the finished mosaic as a guide for placement of the various types of tesserae.

1 Begin by cementing glass coasters (A, B, C), glass nuggets (D, E, F) and ribbon-shaped glass pieces (G) to the table leaf. Be sure to cover the underside of the coasters completely with the adhesive so that the wood is not visible through the glass.

2 On a copy of the pattern, align a sheet of mixed unglazed commercial mosaic tiles (L) over the labeled area. The sheet can be adhered to the table leaf without removing the tiles from the backing but it must be trimmed to fit within the pattern outline. Use a pencil to mark the tiles where they intersect with the design lines.

3 Cut away from the main sheet any tiles that do not fit within the outlined area as well as the tiles that require trimming. Use tile or mosaic nippers to trim the marked tiles along the pencil lines.

4 Apply a thin layer of tile adhesive within the prescribed area. With backing side down, lay trimmed sheet of tiles into position. Using a flat block of wood, press tiles firmly into the adhesive. Place trimmed tiles in the allocated spaces to completely fill the area.

5 Separate enough of the tan (N) and the beige with tan (M) tiles from the net backing to fill the appropriate areas as marked on the pattern. Use the design lines as your guide in determining the adamanto (flow) of the tiles, applying one row at a time. Trim tiles to fit within spaces that are not large enough for an entire tile.

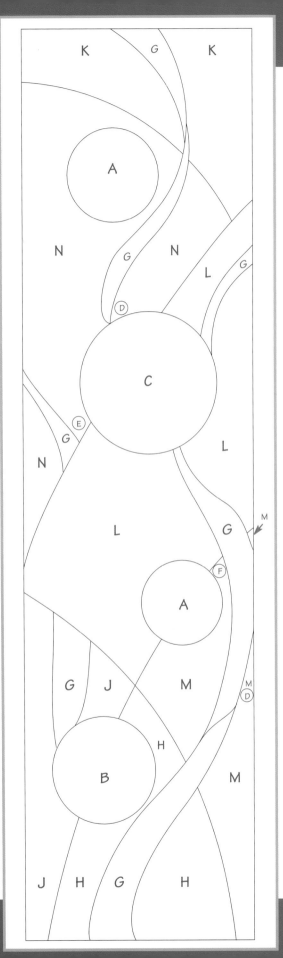

6 Adhere the glass mosaic tiles (H) in the same manner. The mirrored art glass tesserae (J, K) are then glued to the table leaf in the grid-like opus tesselatum style.

7 Because colored grouts may tint or stain porous surfaces, apply a tile sealer to the surface of the unglazed mosaic tiles (L, M, N) before grouting.

8 Complete the mosaic by following the instructions for Applying the Grout (p22) and Cleaning the Finished Piece (p23). A terra-cotta-tinted sanded grout is used to fill the interstices between the tesserae.

NOTE Protect grouted areas of the table leaf from liquids and day-to-day wear by using a grout sealant.

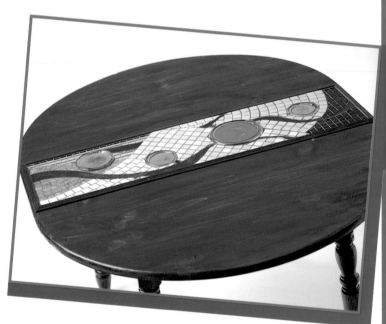

Wizard Mountain

translucent window hanging

Mosaic panel size   25 in wide by 12 in high

Mosaic material required

Letters refer to the type and quantity of art glass used on pattern pieces (p70).
The quantities and types of materials listed are the minimum requirements for completing this project as illustrated, but materials may be substituted, if desired.

A	5 in x 10 in clear with light blue and purple textured streaky
B	3 in x 6 in translucent iridescent amber
C	7 in x 8 in translucent purple with white streaky
D	3 in x 3 in opalescent red with white streaky
E	6 in x 7 in clear with black and white swirls
F	3 in x 4 in blue opal with plum streaky
G	2 in x 3 in translucent light gray
H	15 in x 18 in translucent white, purple and copper red mix
J	12 in x 12 in translucent green, blue and purple streaky
K	5 in x 6 in translucent green, cerise ruby and clear textured streaky
L	translucent red crushed glass frit
M	opaque pink crushed glass frit
N	translucent royal purple crushed glass frit
NOTE	The letter I is not used in this listing.

Base/support structure

A 25 in wide x 12 in high piece of clear granite textured art glass is used as the base for this translucent mosaic window hanging. Refer to Preparing the Base/Support Structure (p27) for general information before starting this project.

There are several ways that this project can be hung. To duplicate the method used in the photograph (pp68, 69), a soldering iron, 60/40 solder, and safety flux are required. Two 30 in lengths of copper re-strip are adhered to the base as both a decorative accent and as a device to hang the mosaic. Re-strip measures $5/32$ in wide and 0.10 in thick and is made from copper and brass.

1   Bend both lengths of copper re-strip to form a right angle at the halfway point.

2   Place the sheet of clear art glass *textured side down* onto a copy of the pattern taped to the work surface. Apply a slim bead of silicone to the glass

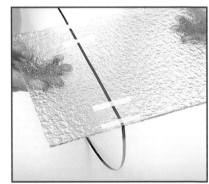

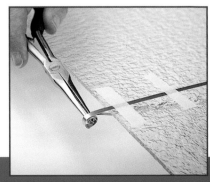

surface along one of the heavy dotted lines, as indicated on the pattern.

3   Lay a length of re-strip flat against the bead of silicone, allowing re-strip to hang over the bottom edge of the glass at the right angle in the middle. Approximately 3 in of re-strip should be extending over the top edge. With a palette knife or craft stick, remove excessive amounts of silicone from either side of the re-strip. Secure re-strip to the glass with several pieces of masking tape and proceed to adhere the second length of re-strip in the same manner. Allow silicone to set for approximately 24 hours.

4   Turn the sheet of glass over. Bend the loose ends of re-strip up and over the bottom edge of the glass and adhere them to the underside as described in steps 2 and 3.

5   Once the silicone has firmly set and the re-strip is adhered securely to the base, the overhanging ends of re-strip can be twisted into loops for hanging. Use a pair of needlenose pliers and devise each loop by rotating the ends of the re-strip down towards the top edge of the glass base. Carefully solder re-strip together to retain the shape of the loop and for additional strength. Do not solder loop closed.

6 Remove the pieces of masking tape used to secure the re-strip to the glass surface while the silicone was setting. Use a utility knife or paint scraper to remove any silicone still visible on either side of the re-strip, taking care not to scratch the glass base. A cloth moistened with isopropyl (rubbing) alcohol will also remove minor traces of silicone. Use dish soap and water to clean the surface of the base and remove any trace of flux residue.

Listed below are three alternatives for hanging this project. Complete the panel following Mosaic Instructions, as listed below, leaving a space marked by heavy dotted lines on the pattern.

• Frame finished mosaic panel as you would a picture but without the backing. The size of the textured glass sheet will have to be increased to allow space around the perimeter to accommodate the framing material.

• Wind heavy-gauge brass wire several times around the base in each of the two spaces marked on the pattern by the heavy dotted line. Twist ends into secure loops for hanging. Glass piece (F) overlaps the dotted line and will have to be shifted over on the design or cut in half and adhered on either side of the line.

• Wrap a length of strong (but decorative) linked metal chain around the completed mosaic in each of the two

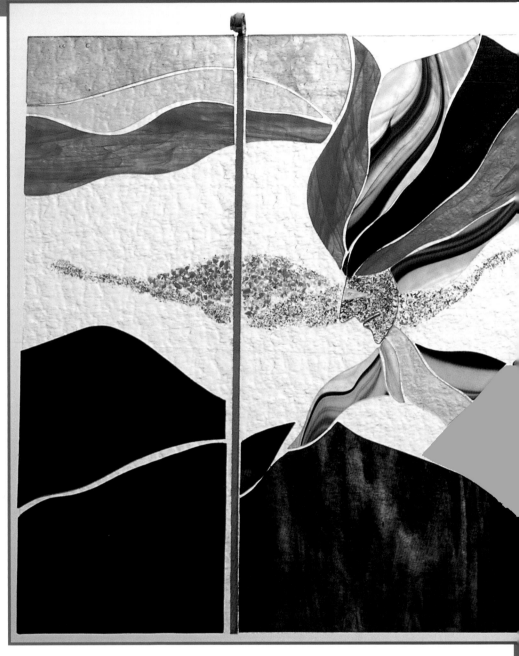

spaces marked on the pattern by the heavy dotted line. Secure the link at one end of the chain to the link located on the opposite side at the top edge of the glass sheet. Hang mosaic from the chain. As previously noted, glass piece (F) must be shifted over or cut in half and adhered on either side of the dotted pattern line.

Mosaic instructions

To construct this mosaic panel follow instructions given for Translucent Mosaics—Basic Steps (p26). Refer to the photograph of the finished mosaic as a guide for placement

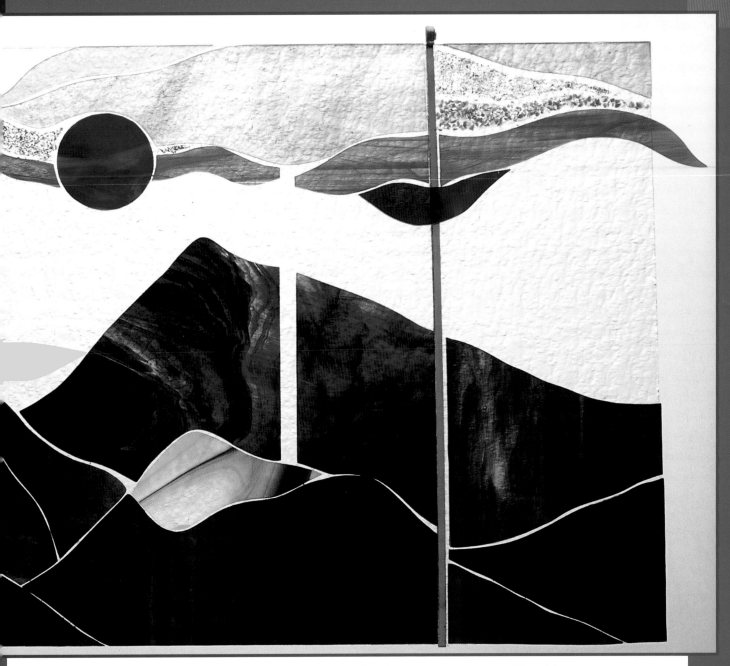

of the various types of tesserae.

1 Butter the entire underside of the shaped glass pieces with a thin layer of silicone and adhere to the base, as indicated on the pattern, one piece at a time. Use a palette knife to remove any silicone that may have oozed out from beneath a glass piece. To maintain an airy, transparent feel, the mosaic will not be grouted. Therefore, pieces can be fitted as closely together as desired. With the exception of piece (C) located at the upper right side of the pattern, none of the glass pieces should extend past the edge of the base. Crushed glass frits are used to create colorful wisps of clouds

(L, M) and to fill in the wizard face (N).

2 Before adhering glass frits, shape a 5 in length of copper re-strip to conform to the outline of the wizard face, as indicated on the pattern by the dotted line. To help secure the metal outline to the glass base, leave a bit of re-strip at either end that can be fitted between the pieces representing the wizard hair (C, E, and J, C).

3 Spread a thin layer of silicone onto the base within the pattern outlines of the wizard face and the adjacent clouds. Smear a bit of silicone on the adjacent edges of the glass pieces that shape his beard (E, G) and the lowest strand of hair (E).

4 Set re-strip outline of face into the silicone on the base, using the pattern copy beneath the glass as a guide. Press ends of the re-strip between the hair pieces (E, J, and C, E) and secure in place with a piece of masking tape, after verifying that the side of the face is resting against the siliconed edge of the lowest strand of hair (E).

5 Place wizard eye (B) in the correct position and cover remaining area with glass frit (N), pressing it gently into the silicone. Secure the outline of his chin against the siliconed edges of the beard (E, G) with a piece of masking tape.

6 Place silicone in the uncovered cloud areas near the top of the base. Sprinkle on the appropriate glass frits (L, M) to create the clouds adjacent to the wizard face, the sun and the upper right corner, covering the areas completely. Use a palette knife to gently press the frits into the silicone.

7 Turn the base over and suspend above a clean sheet of paper. Gently tap the back side to allow excess frits to fall from the surface. The paper sheet saves the frits for later use.

8 Allow silicone to set for at least 24 hours before peeling

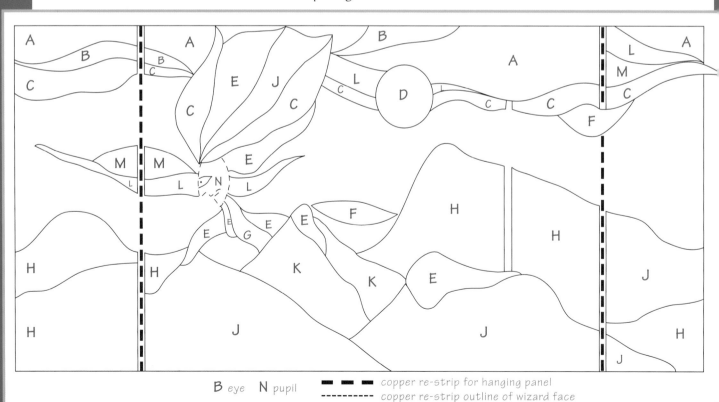

off pieces of masking tape and removing any traces of excess silicone left on the glass surfaces.

9 A protective clear coat can be sprayed over sections covered with glass frits to act as additional fixative. Read and follow the manufacturer's directions carefully and allow silicone to cure for at least 72 hours before applying the protective clear coat. Cover areas that do not require coating with sheets of paper to protect from any overspray.

10 Screw 2 cup hooks into a window frame and suspend the hanging from a length of linked metal chain strong enough to bear the weight of the mosaic.

NOTE

• The edges of each glass piece used in a translucent mosaic are left exposed when grout is not used to fill the interstices. The edges can be smoothed (p19) with a diamond pad or wet/dry sandpaper. Whenever possible, glide each glass edge against a mirror grinding bit to achieve a more polished edge with less effort.

• *See* note (p54) for how to make frits.

• *See* safety reminder (p54).

B eye   N pupil

▬ ▬ ▬ copper re-strip for hanging panel

- - - - - - - - copper re-strip outline of wizard face

Deco Fireplace

Create a mosaic facade for a fireplace to complement and blend with the room decor. This design is in the art deco style but it can be adapted to suit any taste and circumstances.

About this project

Specific measurements and material listings for this project are not provided because of the great variations of style and size of individual fireplaces. Consult local professionals when choosing mosaic materials for your particular fireplace installation.

The design is a series of scalloped shapes using several shades of ivory art glass for the background tesserae and black art glass for the larger pattern shapes and the border trim around the fireplace unit, the hearth, and along the sides. Small bits of red art glass are inserted randomly to add color. The hearth is covered by a large black art glass tile, measuring 4 in x 4 in, surrounded by 2 in x 2 in square tiles cut from opaque green and caramel art glass with 4 black accent tiles of the same size.

Refer to the photograph (p73) of the finished mosaic and the overall pattern (p72) as a guide for drawing the pattern and for placement of the tesserae. The pattern shapes for the tesserae can be adjusted to accommodate any particular requirements. After measuring the area to be tessellated, draw pattern on graph paper to determine the size and number of tesserae required. Remember to leave at least $\frac{1}{16}$ in space between the tesserae. Once the pattern is complete and the surface of the base prepared (p21), draw sight lines on the base to aid in the accurate positioning of the tesserae, as shown in the photograph. The pieces are applied following basic guidelines given for the Direct Method (p20) of mosaic construction.

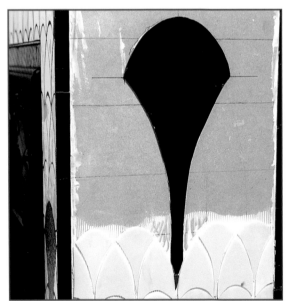

Base/support structure

The mosaic surround and hearth for this project are made for an electric fireplace unit. This particular unit does not generate much heat so the base is constructed from high-density particle board. For most wood burning and natural gas fueled fireplaces the surrounding base should be made of noncombustible heat-resistant materials.

Mosaic materials

Art glass is used to make the tesserae that surround the electric fireplace unit and cover the hearth. Almost any glass or ceramic-based material can be used to create a fireplace mosaic as long as it is nonflammable and heat tolerant. When putting together a mosaic for a wood burning fireplace, use a heavy-duty durable tile to cover the hearth. A thick tile (ceramic, stone, marble, etc.) that is impact-resistant and tolerant of heat can resist damage caused by falling logs, fireplace tools, heat from the fire, etc.

Adhesives and grouts

Use nonflammable heat-resistant adhesives and cement-based grouts when assembling the mosaic panel around a fireplace. Avoid the use of organic tile mastics that may be flammable and intolerant of heat. This project uses a charcoal-tinted sanded grout to fill the interstices between the tesserae and accentuate the glass selection.

NOTE

• When covering the hearth with tile or tesserae, leave $\frac{1}{4}$ in space between the floor and the edge of the mosaic. This clearance will allow for any seasonal movement in the building. The space can be filled with a bead of silicone if desired.

• Verify with local authorities that all materials and fireplace unit are compliant with fire codes and regulations.

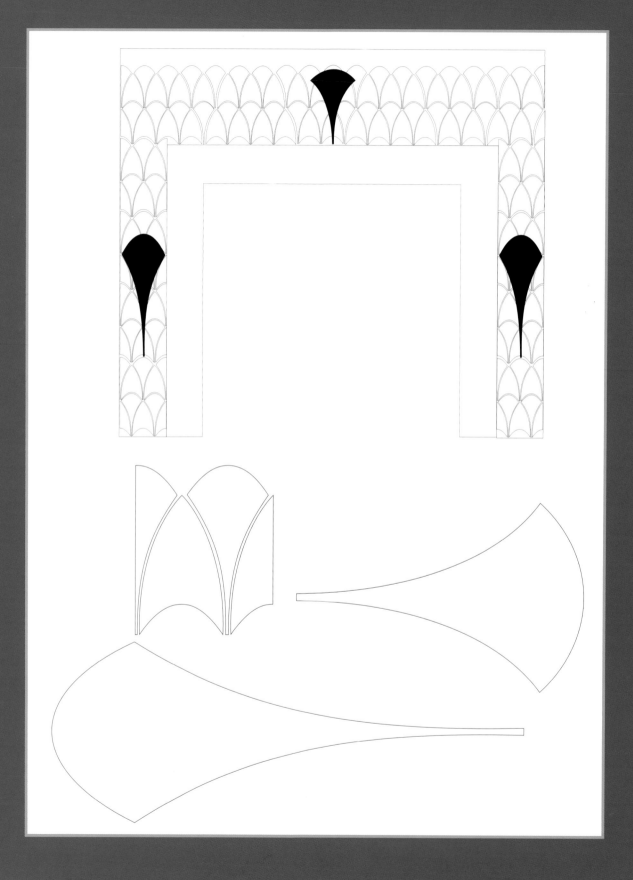

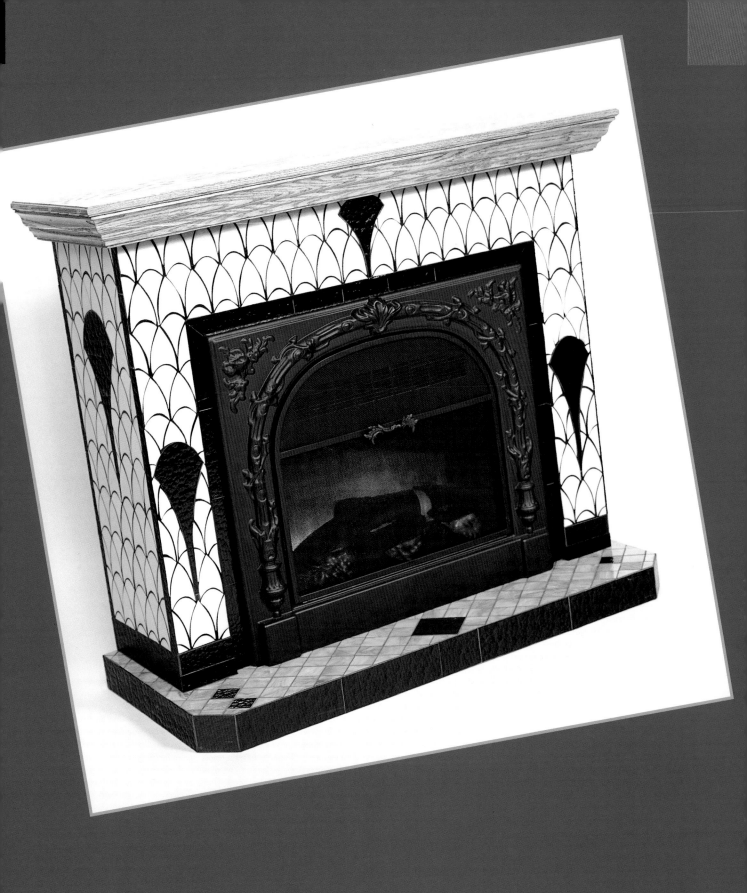

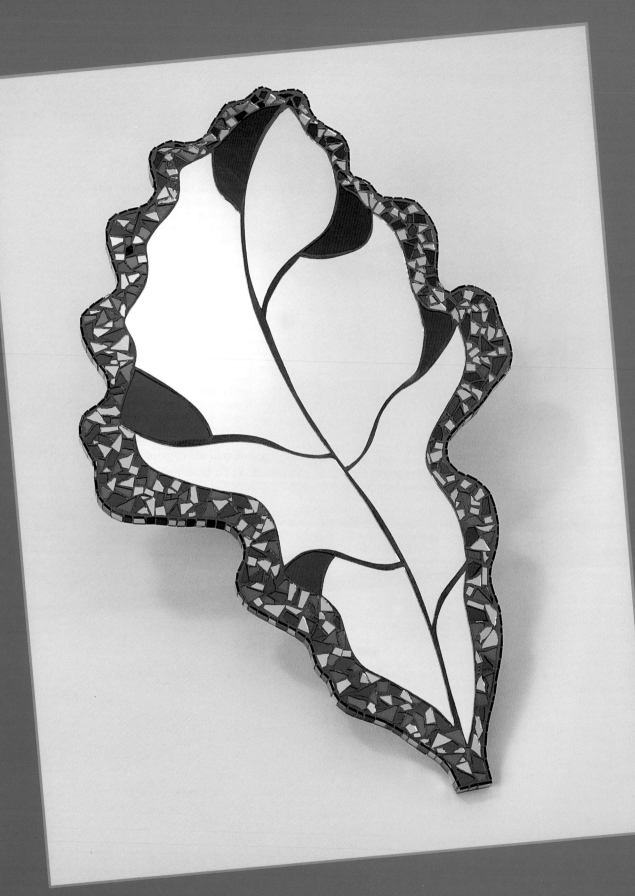

Autumn Oak Leaf

wall mirror

Mosaic panel size   33½ in by 20½ in high

Mosaic material required

Letters refer to the type and quantity of mosaic material used on pattern pieces (p76).
The quantities and types of materials listed are the minimum requirements for completing this project as illustrated, but materials may be substituted, if desired.

A   18 in x 32 in 3mm mirror
B   8 in x 14 in mirrored dark amber semi-antique art glass
C   6 in x 8 in mirrored light amber semi-antique art glass
D   6 in x 8 in mirrored dark green semi-antique art glass
E   6 in x 8 in mirrored light green semi-antique art glass

Base/support structure

Guidelines for constructing a base/support structure are given in Making Wood Base/Support Structures for Mosaic Panels and Wall Hangings (p28). Specific instructions for this project are as follows:

1   Trace the perimeter of the oak leaf outline onto a 36 in X 24 in piece of ¾ in exterior grade plywood.

2   Using a jigsaw, cut out base along the traced outline.

3   Sand edges smooth with sandpaper.

4   Trace all design lines from pattern copy onto the base and key (score) plywood surface with a utility knife to aid adhesion.

Mosaic instructions

This wall mirror is constructed following instructions given for the Direct Method (p20) of mosaic construction. Refer to the photograph of the finished mosaic as a guide for placement of the various types of tesserae.

1   Cut (p11) the larger shaped pieces (A, B) that form the central leaf design of the mirror. Smooth (p19) the edges where necessary. If possible, use a mirror grinding bit to finish the edges of each piece.

2   Adhere these pieces to the base with neutral curing silicone, mirror mastic, or a non-corrosive tile adhesive. These products will not affect the silver backing of the mirror. Allow to cure as per the manufacturer's instructions and follow any safety precautions listed.

3   Cover these larger pieces with a

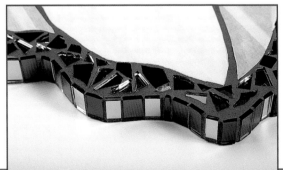

layer of overlapping rows of masking tape to protect surface.

4   From a piece (approximately 2 in x 8 in) of each of the mirrored semi-antique art glasses (B, C, D, E), use glass mosaic or tile cutters to make random-size tesserae.

5   In random color order, adhere the tesserae to the base as indicated on the pattern. Use a non-corrosive tile adhesive and leave a ¹⁄₁₆ in allowance between the edge of the tesserae and the edge of the base to allow the application of a border row of tesserae.

6   Cut the remaining sheets of mirrored semi-antique art glass (B, C, D, E) into ¾ in strips. Cut each strip into rectangular tesserae ranging in width from ¼ in to ¾ in.

7   With the base lying flat on the work surface, glue the tesserae along the edge of the base approximately ¹⁄₁₆ in apart and in random color order. Choose each tessera for an appropriate width to fit along the irregular and curving shape of the base.

8   Once the adhesive has cured, complete the project following directions given for Applying the Grout (p22) and Cleaning the Finished Piece (p23). A terra-cotta-tinted sanded grout is used to fill the interstices between the tesserae of this project.

9   Remove masking tape from larger pieces once the mirror has been completed.

10   Refer to Mounting Wall Hangings, Plaques, and Mirrors (p29) for instructions on hanging the finished mosaic. The irregular shape of this mirror allows it to be

hung at any angle.

NOTE

• Sanded grout is gritty and may scratch mirrored surfaces even after it has cured. Use a grout sealer to keep sand particles affixed between the interstices. Or, substitute a smooth non-sanded grout for the sanded version.

• When working with larger pieces of mirrored glass, always cut mirror on the glass side, not the silvered underside.

• Small chips may appear in the silvering along the edge of a mirror if a piece requires grinding or shaping to fit the pattern. These chips can be visible once the mirror is in place and can mar the appearance of the mosaic. Chips can be removed or lessened by smoothing the silvered edge at a 45° angle using a glass grinder, wet/dry sandpaper, diamond pad, or carborundum stone. Refer to Smoothing Jagged and Sharp Edges on Mosaic Pieces (p19) for specific instructions about tools and techniques.

• To prevent discoloration or damage to the silver backing, use a neutral curing silicone, mirror mastic, or a non-corrosive tile adhesive to glue the mirrored pieces to the base.

• Cover the mirror surface with a single layer of overlapping rows of masking tape to prevent scratches while applying other tesserae and/or sanded grout.

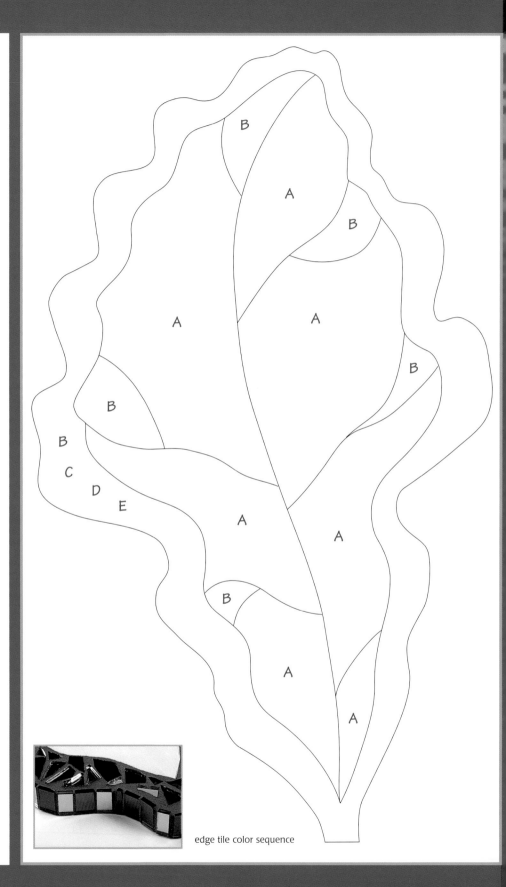

edge tile color sequence

Fish Pond

tabletop

Mosaic panel size   irregular circular shape approximately 26 in diameter

Mosaic material required

Letters refer to the type and quantity of mosaic material used on pattern pieces (p80).
The quantities and types of materials listed are the minimum requirements for completing this project as illustrated, but materials may be substituted, if desired.

A	12 in x 12 in medium green ring mottle art glass
B	6 in x 6 in light green with white streaky art glass
C	6 in x 6 in opaque orange with white streaky art glass
D	6 in x 6 in opaque white art glass
E	6 in x 6 in translucent white with coral and pink streaky art glass
F	6 in x 6 in opaque white with orange streaky art glass
G	6 in x 12 in translucent red with opaque white streaky art glass
H	6 in x 12 in translucent orange red with white streaky art glass
J	6 in x 6 in translucent cranberry art glass
K	12 in x 18 in iridescent clear heavy ripple textured art glass
L	6 in x 12 in translucent iridescent light blue heavy ripple textured art glass
M	assorted pebbles and small rocks to cover an area approximately 3 sq ft plus 1 cup of sand

NOTE the letter I is not used in this listing.

Base/support structure

This mosaic tabletop has a translucent mosaic panel in the center of a wood base that is covered with pebbles, rocks, and sand. Base/support structure instructions:

1 Trace the outline of the tabletop perimeter onto a 30 in x 30 in piece of ¾ in exterior grade plywood.

2 Using a jigsaw, cut out base piece along the traced outline.

3 Center a sheet of carbon paper and a copy of the pattern over the tabletop surface and trace the outline of the opening with a hard-tipped pen or pencil.

4 Using a jigsaw, cut out along the *inside* of the traced outline of the pond area and remove the plywood center from the base piece.

5 On the top surface of the base piece, use a router to make a ⅜ in rabbet (right-angled groove) along the edge of the pond cutout. This is where the translucent mosaic panel will be inserted.

6 Sand smooth any rough edges along the outside and cutout edges of the tabletop.

7 Using the plywood cutout piece

as a template, trace the outline onto a sheet of graph paper. Measure and draw a second outline that is ⁵⁄₁₆ in wide around the perimeter of the traced pond shape. With scissors or a utility knife, cut out this new and larger outline. This is the template for the 6mm clear glass base for the translucent mosaic panel.

8 The template must fit within the pond cutout and overlap onto the recessed edge by at least ¼ in. Make adjustments to the template if necessary.

9 With a permanent waterproof marker, trace the outline of the template onto a piece of 6mm clear float glass approximately 22 in x 22 in. Cut out (p11) the piece. Place

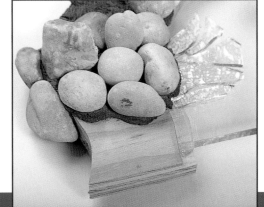

the shaped glass piece into the recessed opening to verify an accurate fit. Grind (p19) or groze (p19) any glass edge that is too large for the opening. Once a satisfactory fit is achieved, smooth (p19) any rough edges.

10 Set the wood base face up on the work surface. Squeeze a slim bead of silicone into the corner of the recessed groove around the entire perimeter of the opening. Place glass piece into the opening and press gently onto the silicone bead.

11 Allow the silicone to set completely for approximately 24 hours. Use a utility knife or razor blade to remove any silicone that may have oozed from between the wood base and the glass piece.

12 Key the wood surface and clean the glass with soap and water. Apply a weatherproofing sealant to the underside of the wood portion of the base.

Mosaic instructions

Assemble the mosaic portion of the Fish Pond tabletop using a combination of the Direct Method (p20) and the techniques described in Translucent Mosaics–Basic Steps (p26). Refer to the photograph of the finished mosaic as a guide for placement of the various types of tesserae.

1 Follow instructions given for Translucent Mosaics (p26). Cut the glass required to form the koi fish (C to J) and the lily pads (A, B) into small and medium random-shaped tesserae. The tesserae used to represent water (K, L) should be a mixture of medium and large random shapes. Adhere glass tesserae to the top surface of the glass base piece using clear silicone as the adhesive. Leave ½ in space around the perimeter of the glass base piece free of tesserae and silicone. Pebbles and rocks will be applied to the wood framework of the base and will overlap onto

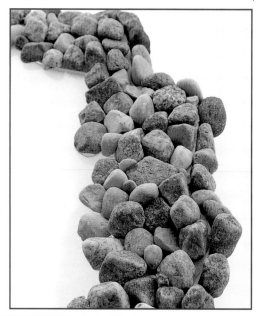

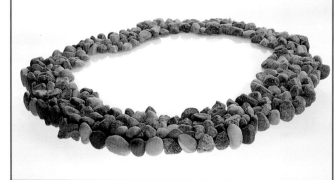

the glass surface to camouflage the area where the wood ends and the glass surface starts. Scrape away excess silicone from the edges of the tesserae.

2 After the silicone has set completely, grout (pp22, 23) the translucent mosaic pond using thin-set mortar. For greater water-resistance and weatherproofing, choose a thin-set mortar mix and substitute latex polymer additive for the water required. Read and follow the manufacturer's instructions carefully. Remove any excess mortar from the perimeter of the glass base piece.

3 Thin-set mortar is used as both the adhesive and the grout to complete the area surrounding the pond. Prepare enough mortar to cover approximately one-quarter to one-half of the surface of the wood portion of the base at one time. Mix to a thick, smooth, and creamy consistency. Allow the mixture to stand for approximately 10 minutes.

4 With a small trowel or rubber spatula, spread a layer of the wet mortar mix (approximately 1/16 in to 1/8 in thick) over a section of the wood surface. Do not spread mortar on more area than can be covered with the pebbles and rocks in 15 minutes. Press pebbles and rocks firmly into the mortar, placing them in a random fashion and fitting them closely together. Cover the entire top surface of the base, overlapping onto the uncovered perimeter of the glass base piece and up to the edge of the attached glass tesserae.

5 Place several blocks of wood under the outer rim of the tabletop to elevate it slightly over the work surface. Cover exposed wood edges of the base with pebbles and rocks, adhering them with thin-set mortar. Allow rocks to overhang edge just enough to conceal the base completely. Wipe away excess mortar with a damp sponge and then allow the mortar to set completely for at least 24 hours before grouting.

6 Following instructions for Applying the Grout (pp22, 23), fill crevices between the pebbles and rocks using the same thin-set mortar mix as used to adhere them. Sprinkle sand over the damp, freshly applied thin-set mortar for a more realistic look. Lightly press sand into the grout surface with a damp sponge before allowing the grout to set as usual.

7 Clean finished surface with a damp sponge and then buff with a dry cloth. A paint scraper or utility knife can be used to scrape away any unwanted dry mortar that will not

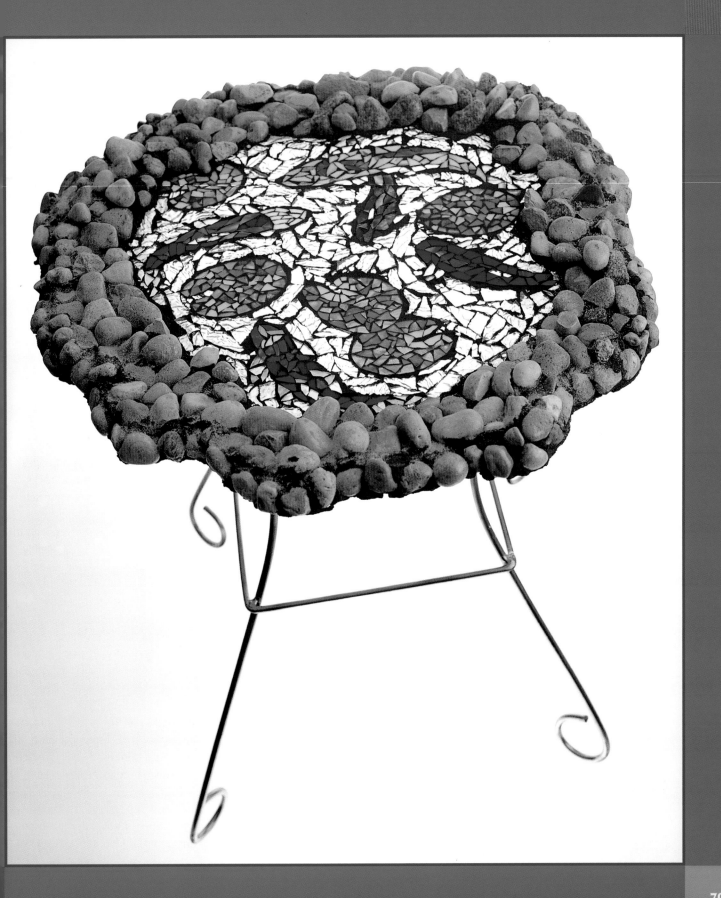

buff off. Toothbrushes and dental picks can also be used to remove unwanted mortar.

8 The tabletop, as illustrated in the photograph, is secured onto a custom-made metal frame. Many ready-made stands can be used to support the tabletop or make one yourself.

9 Allow tabletop to fully cure for several days before placing it outdoors.

NOTE

• Iridescent clear and light blue ripple textured glass tesserae (K, L) create a rippling and shimmering effect to represent glints of sunshine reflecting off ripples of water. To accomplish this be sure to adhere the tesserae with the textured side facing upwards.

• Consider using glass nuggets to make interesting accents resembling water bubbles.

• To illuminate the tabletop at night, aim a beam from an outdoor spotlight so that the light strikes the underside of the translucent mosaic in the center.

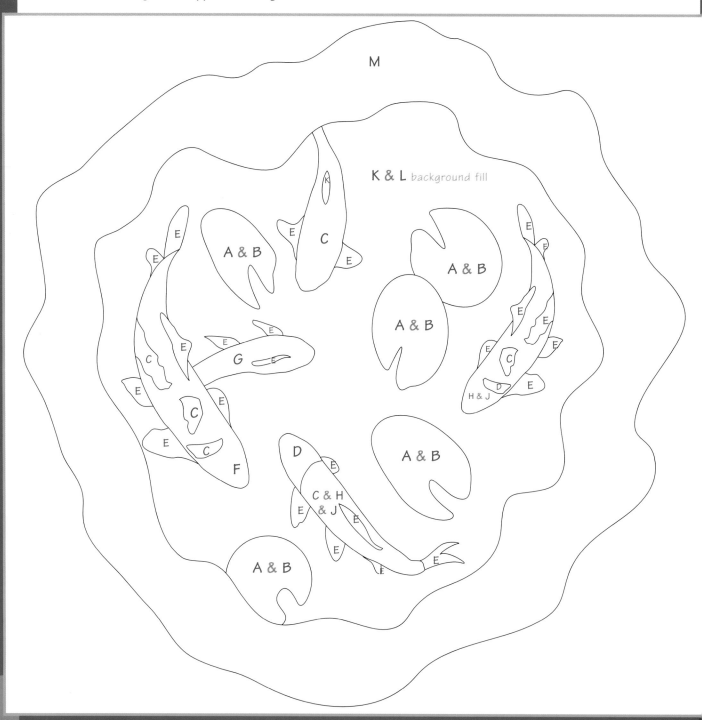

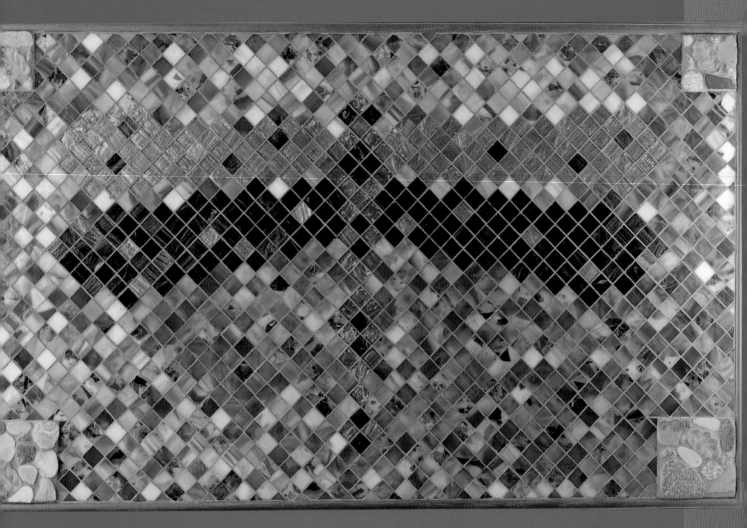

Dream of the Dragonfly

large wall hanging

Mosaic panel size   37½ in wide by 22 in high

Mosaic material required

Letters refer to the type and quantity of mosaic material used on pattern pieces (p83).

The quantities and types of materials listed are the minimum requirements for completing this project as illustrated, but materials may be substituted, if desired.

- A   29—¾ in x ¾ in translucent green and copper glass mosaic tiles
- B   127—¾ in x ¾ in translucent copper glass mosaic tiles
- C   159—¾ in x ¾ in translucent brown and copper glass mosaic tiles
- D   5 sq ft cobalt and white with green and brown fractures art glass (cut into ¾ in x ¾ in tesserae)
- E   assorted rocks and pebbles
- F   4 translucent amber glass leaves

Base/support structure

Guidelines for constructing a base/support structure with wood trim molding are given in Making Wood Base/Support Structures for Mosaic Panels and Wall Hangings (p28).

Mosaic instructions

This mosaic panel was constructed using a combination of the Indirect Method (p23) and the Direct Method (p20) of mosaic construction. Because of the size and nature of the design the indirect method is used to assemble the multitude of tesserae thus saving time by not having to transfer the pattern's extensive grid onto the base and by enabling large sections of mosaic to be adhered in a matter of minutes. Assorted rocks, pebbles (E) and glass leaves (F) vary in size, shape, and thickness, and therefore are affixed one at a time directly to the base. Refer to the photograph of the finished mosaic as a guide for placement of the various types of tesserae.

1 When preparing the base/support structure, place carbon paper and a copy of the pattern over the top surface of the base. Use a hard-tipped pen or pencil to mark guidelines to make aligning and adhering the various sections of mosaic easier and more accurate:

• Trace the outline of the 4 corner areas where assorted rocks (E) and glass leaves (F) will be placed.

• Measure and mark a center line that runs from top to bottom onto the base. On this line, mark the positions indicating the top of the head and the end of the tail. Use this line to center the dragonfly body on the base when adhering the mosaic.

• Extend a horizontal line from each wing tip to the adjacent edge of the base using the pattern grid as a guide.

2 Once all sections of tesserae have been adhered to the base and the adhesive has fully cured, carefully peel back adhesive-backed vinyl to reveal the surface of the mosaic.

3 Then using the Direct Method (p20), fill in the vacant corner spaces by gluing assorted rocks and pebbles (E) and glass leaves (F) to the base.

4 Complete the mosaic by Applying the Grout (p22) and Cleaning the Finished Piece (p23). A sand-tinted sanded grout is used to fill the interstices between the tesserae.

5 Refer to Mounting Wall Hangings, Plaques, and Mirrors (p29) for instructions on hanging the finished mosaic.

NOTE

• The underside of art glass sheet D (for background tesserae) is covered with thin pieces of green and brown glass known as fractures. This beautiful handmade glass is often used in stained glass lamps and panels to represent areas of distant and muted foliage. Add depth and interest to the background of this mosaic panel by turning over some of the tesserae and adhering them to the base with the reverse (fracture) side up.

• When smaller tesserae are required for a project, it is often easier to cut a larger tessera into the smaller pieces required. Make the triangular tesserae that are along the perimeter of the mosaic panel by cutting the background tesserae (D) in half diagonally, creating two triangular pieces.

• Found objects such as the translucent amber glass leaves (F) used in this project can make an ordinary mosaic more picturesque. Visit local gift boutiques, craft shops, and home decorating stores when looking for novel and unusual accent pieces.

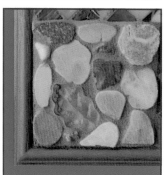

• To add an earthy texture to the grouted corner areas, sprinkle sand over the damp, freshly applied grout. Lightly press the sand into the grout surface with a damp sponge before allowing the grout to set as usual.

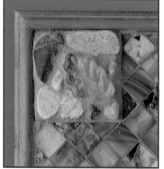

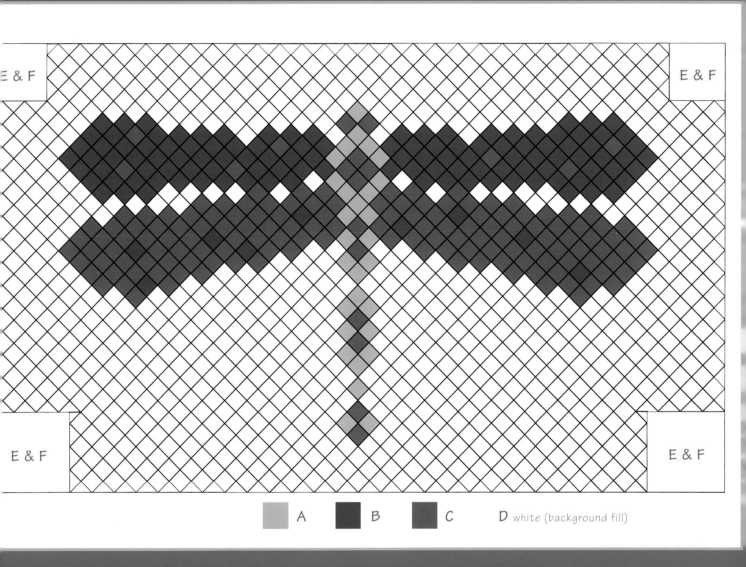

E & F

E & F

E & F

E & F

A   B   C   D white (background fill)

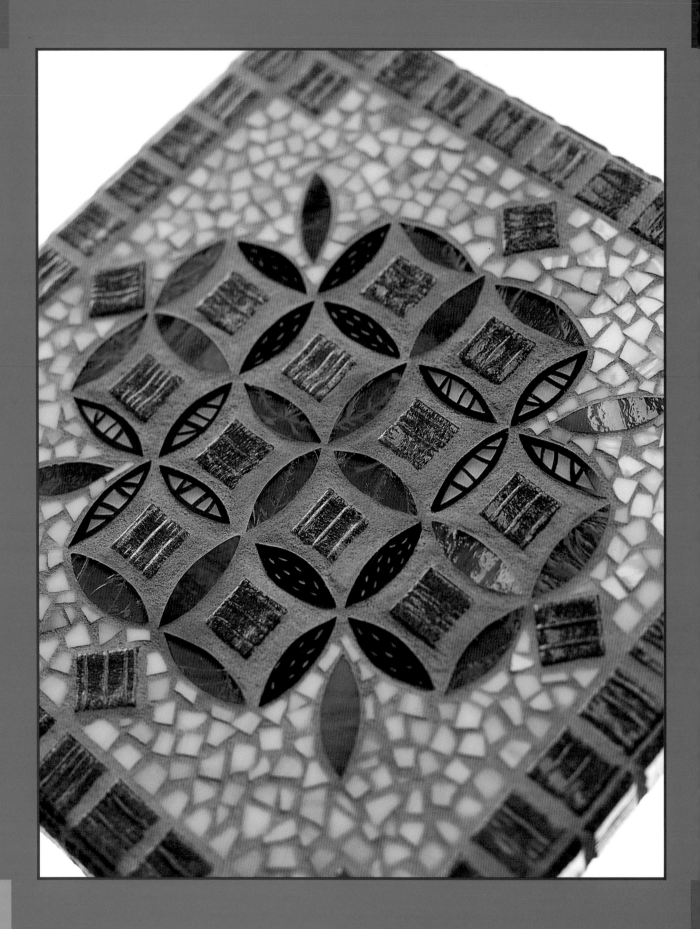

Wedding Quilt

small wall hanging

Mosaic panel size   **10 in square**

Mosaic material required

Letters refer to the type and quantity of mosaic material used on pattern pieces (p86).
The quantities and types of materials listed are the minimum requirements for completing this project as illustrated, but materials may be substituted, if desired.

- A   112—¾ in x ¾ in grape vitreous glass mosaic tiles
- B   2 in x 8 in translucent red glue chip art glass
- C   2 in x 6 in opaque red with white streaky art glass
- D   4 in x 6 in translucent dark red art glass
- E   5 in x 8 in opaque pale purple with white wisps art glass (cut into small random-size tesserae)

Base/support structure

1 piece 10 in x 10 in—¾ in exterior grade plywood

Mosaic instructions

This mosaic panel can be fabricated using either the Direct Method (p20) or the Indirect Method (p23) of mosaic construction. Choose the method you prefer. Refer to the photograph of the finished mosaic as a guide for placement of the various types of tesserae.

1   Adhere mosaic tiles (A) and cut glass tesserae (B, C, D) that form the central design motif to the base.

2   Before filling in the background areas with random-size tesserae (E), adhere a border row of mosaic tiles (A). Leave a space approximately ¹⁄₁₆ in around mosaic perimeter to ensure tesserae do not protrude over the edge of the base.

3   Lay base flat on work surface and adhere glass mosaic tiles (A) along the outside edge of the plywood. Each of the four sides will require 12 tiles evenly spaced approximately ¹⁄₁₆ in apart. Allow adhesive to set for approximately 24 hours.

4   Using a pale mauve-tinted sanded grout, follow instructions for Applying the Grout (p22) to fill interstices between tesserae.

5   Refer to Cleaning the Finished Piece (p23) and Mounting Wall Hangings, Plaques, and Mirrors (p29) prior to hanging the finished piece.

NOTE

• Turn over art glass pieces (B) and mosaic tiles (A) and apply to the base with the textured underside up to add interest and texture to the smooth top surface.

• For those glass artisans with sandblasting skills and equipment, additional decorative elements can be added to several tesserae (D) by etching the surface. Use red on clear flashed full-antique art glass and sandblast away portions of the red flashing to create interesting patterns.

• The wide grout-filled spaces between the tesserae in the center of the mosaic panel form an integral part of the overall design. This area may require grouting more than once to achieve an even finish. Use sanded grout and allow the grout to cure at a slower rate to prevent cracking. Place a small sheet of plastic over the area and lightly mist with water occasionally to slow the drying time.

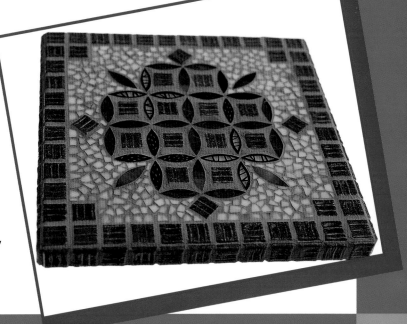

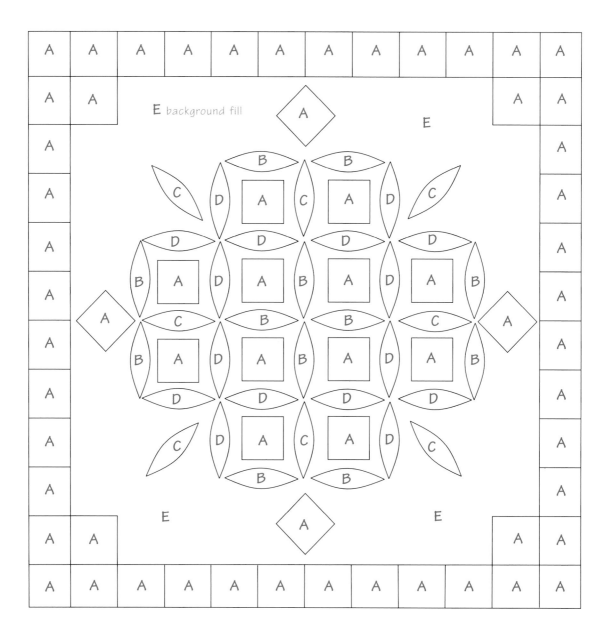

Mosaic
Ideas

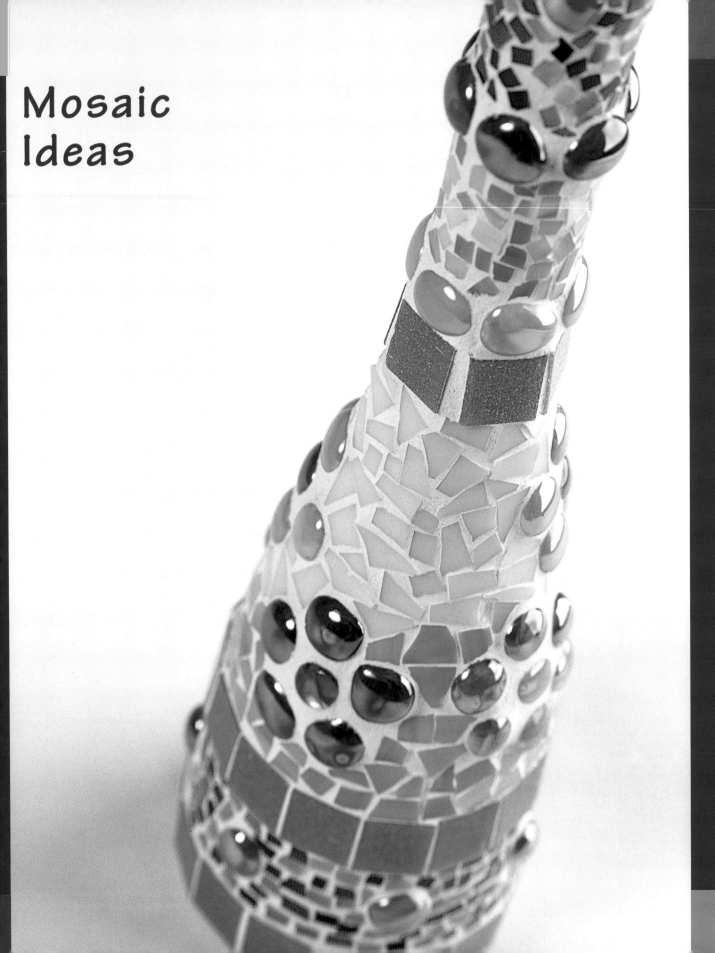

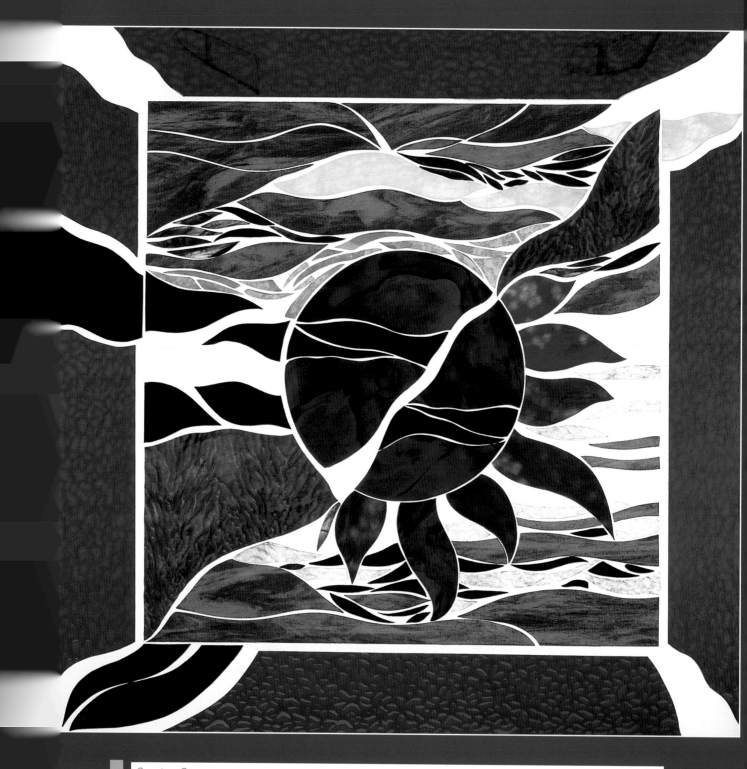

Sunrise, Sunset
This contemporary translucent panel expands on traditional mosaic techniques by transmitting light rather than reflecting it off the surface of the tesserae. Bold and complex shapes cut from art glasses create a new and different dynamic not achievable when using traditional square tesserae and materials.

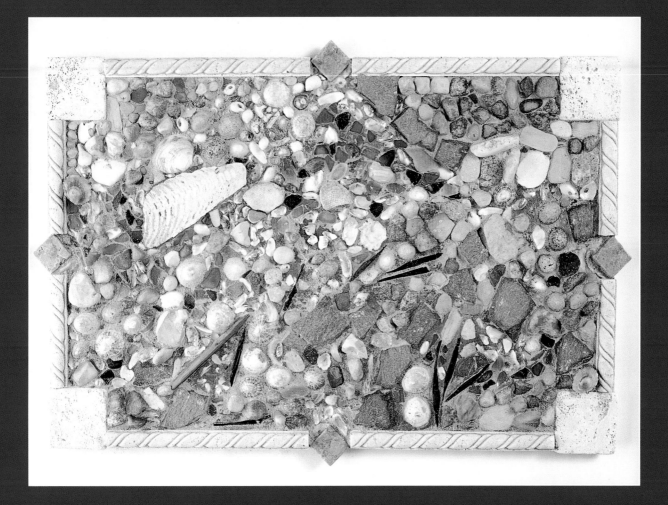

Antiquity

Found objects and articles collected on family vacations replace traditional tesserae materials. Project uses direct method (p20) and materials and handfuls of sand are imbedded in thin-set mortar spread over the surface of the support structure. Memorabilia used here: sea shells, beach glass and pebbles, fossils, pieces of antler, and beach sand.

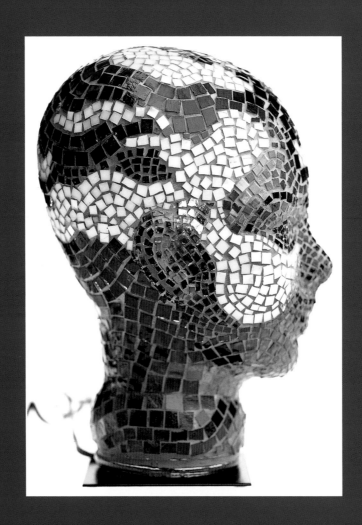

Dream Weaver
Illuminated sculpture created by adhering rows of translucent art glass tesserae to a hollow glass display fixture. Tesserae fashioned into abstract cloud shapes and applied using opus vermiculatum method (p22). Mosaic is illuminated from within by a low-wattage bulb or a metal base.

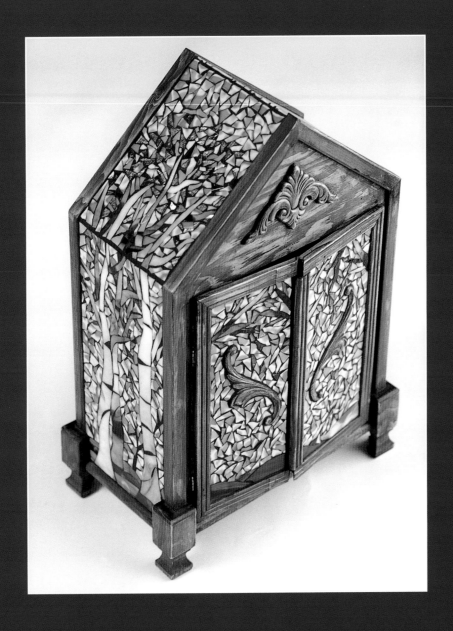

Safe Place

Panels depict a magical birch forest. Tree trunks and branches are cut and shaped from art glass; leaves formed by cutting a variety of glass mosaic tiles into random shaped pieces using tile nippers. Indirect method is used to assemble pieces on clear adhesive-backed vinyl; background filled in with randomly shaped art glass tesserae and then adhered to cabinet with ceramic tile adhesive.

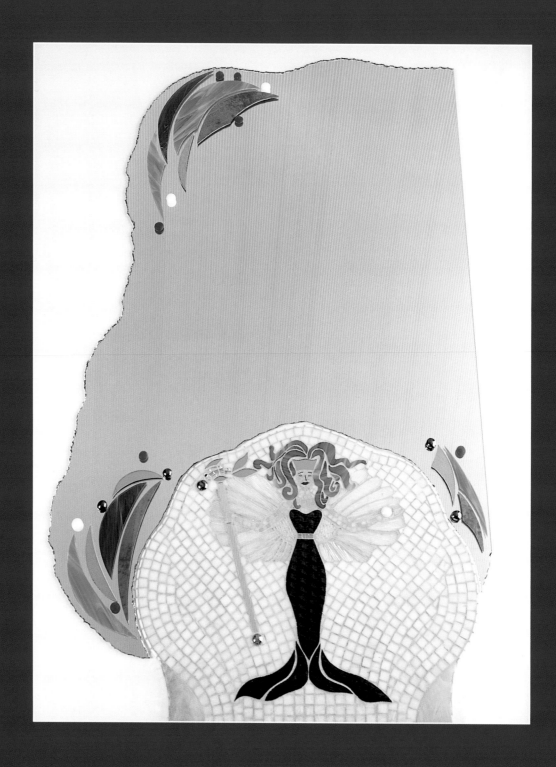

Floor & Mirror Installation 1

Bathroom mirror ties together floor installation and mosaic back splash. Back splash uses traditional direct method (p20) and a sheet of mirror is cut to frame the shell-shaped outline. Glass nuggets and swirls of art glass are adhered to mirror and floor installation. Mirror is not grouted.

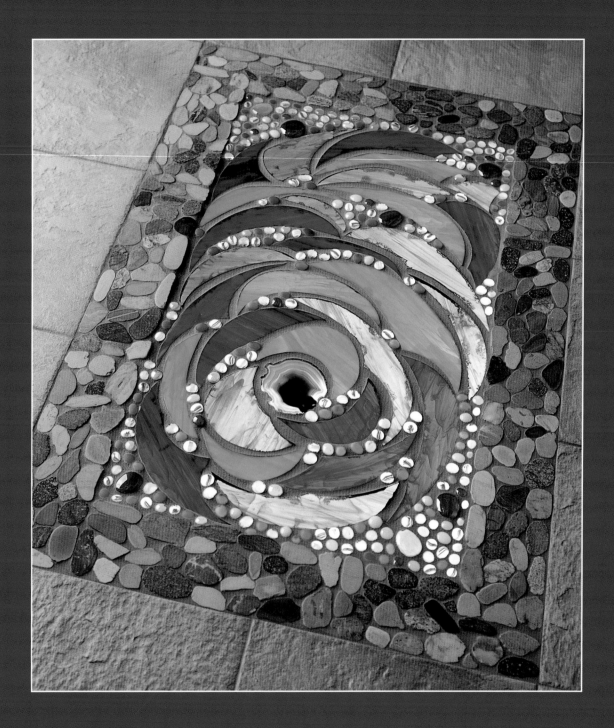

Floor & Mirror Installation 2

Illuminated translucent mosaic panel is inlaid into a ceramic tile floor. Panel assembled on ¾ in clear float glass, illuminated by a light box beneath the floor. Colorful glass nuggets outline swirling shapes in blue and green art glasses that surround a blue geode. Wide grout lines accent glass pieces. Frame panel in a border of thinly sliced rocks and pebbles.

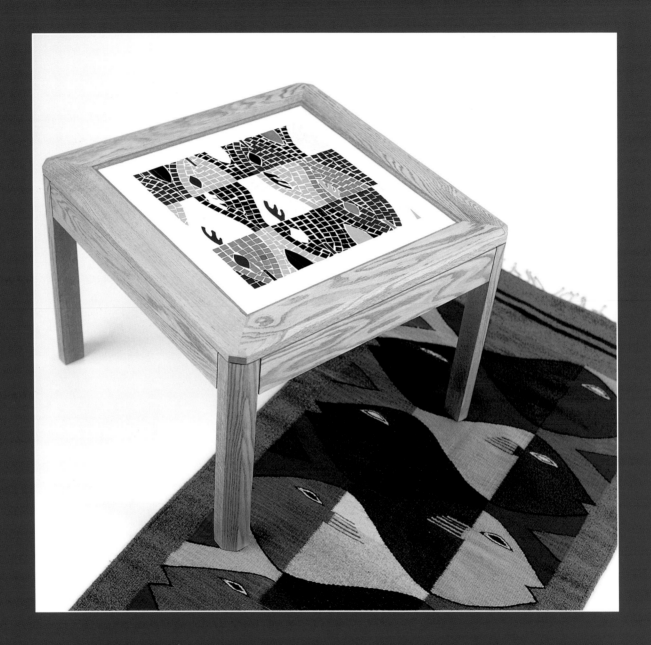

Piscean

Ideas for making your own mosaic designs can come from a variety of sources. Stencil and clipart books, fabric swatches, and traditional design motifs are but a few of an endless list of possible inspirations. Pattern for this mosaic is influenced by the aquatic theme in a woven wool rug. Tesserae for tabletop can be assembled using either the direct or indirect methods of mosaic construction.

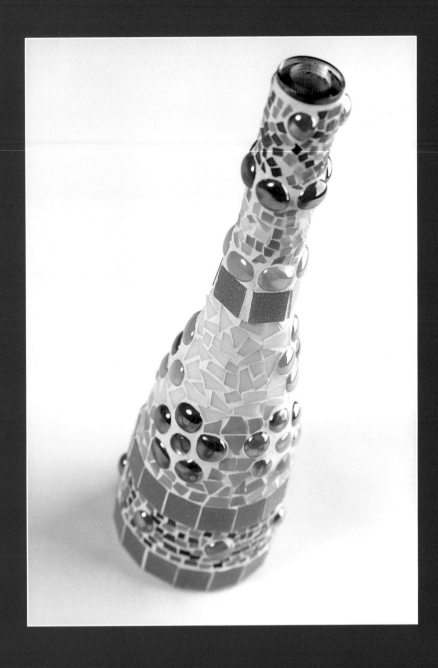

Daisy
Glass bottles make inexpensive and ready-made base/support structures. Cover with mosaics for contemporary or classic vase.

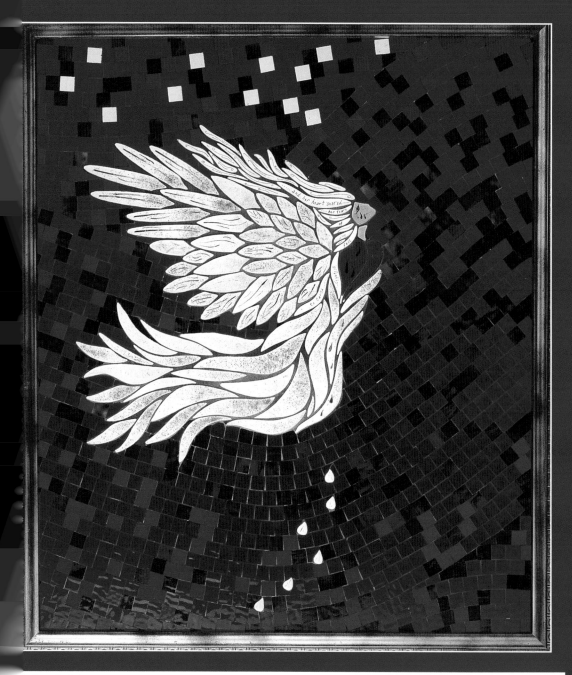

aring Spirit

male figure and falling teardrops in this translucent window panel are created entirely from
ndmade glass tiles. Each tile has 2 layers of shaped compatible clear glass, fired in a kiln until pieces
e together to form a single unit. Crushed glass frits and pieces of 22 karat gold leaf are sandwiched
ween the layers of glass to add color. Decorative details are hand painted in yellow and white gold
d permanently fired onto the top surface of the shaped tiles. Background is handcut square glass
serae in cobalt blue and cranberry. A sheet of 6mm clear float glass framed with wide, sturdy picture
ldings is the base piece. Use clear silicone to adhere tesserae. Grout is muted mauve-tinted.

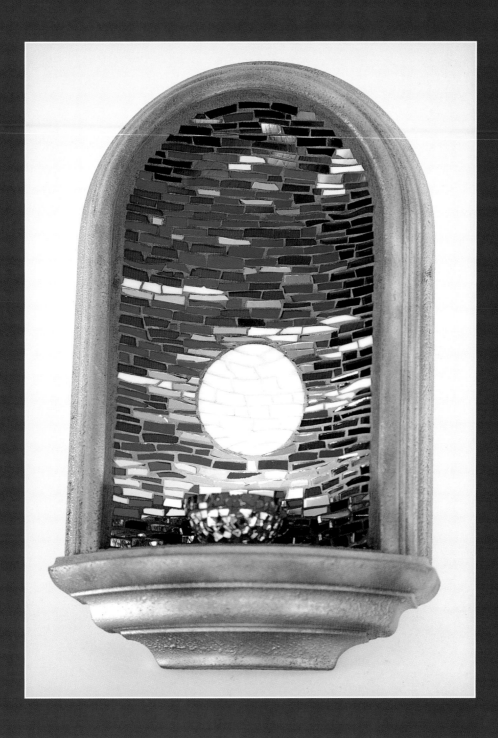

Nocturne

Use architectural fixtures as objects for innovative base/support structures for mosaic works. This niche is covered with mirrored semi-antique glasses in shades of blue and purple. Light interest is created by candle that reflects off the surface of the mirrored tesserae.

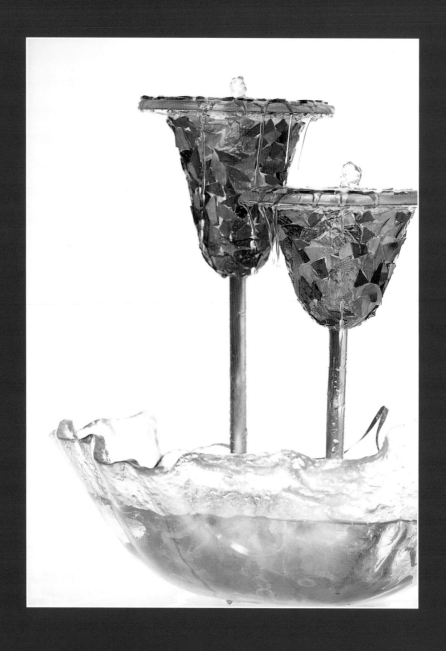

Autumn Falls (side view)

Contemporary indoor waterfall is created utilizing glass working and mosaic techniques. Large clear bowl is kiln-formed in an organic shape to hold the water and the waterfall apparatus. A small bowl inside large bowl is covered with translucent glass tesserae and houses water pump. Copper pipe carries the water to the elevated slumped glass water basins. The large

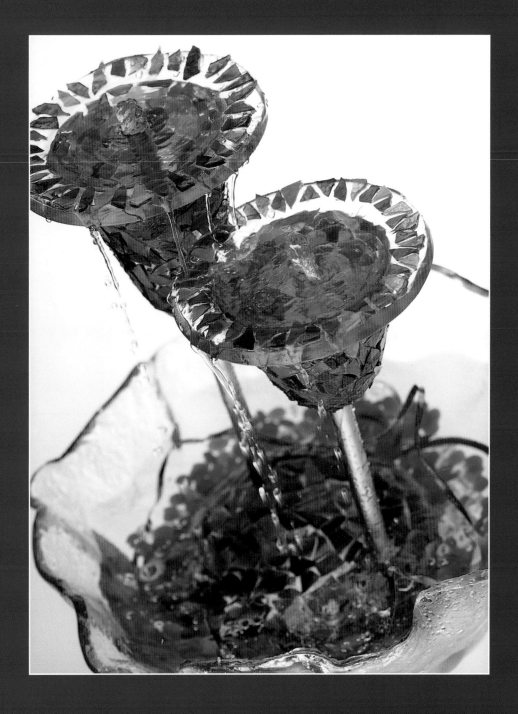

Autumn Falls (view from the top)

gaps between the tesserae around the rims of the water basins divert the overflow of water to make eye-catching display. Glass nuggets lie at the bottom of large bowl and copper strips twist and undulate in the water.

Mosaic Garden & Patio Stones

Try giving a new look to your garden this year.

Mosaic garden stones add charm and definition around flower beds, walkways, fish ponds, and patios.

Choose a pattern with a bright color scheme that complements your garden
and adds a touch of color during the transition
from one blooming period to the next.

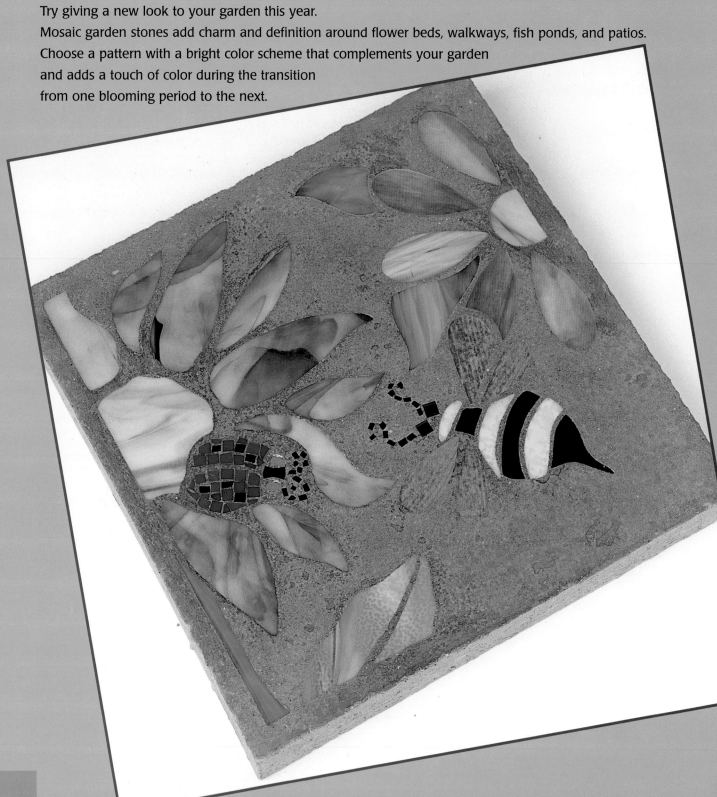

Basic Steps

Materials

3 copies of pattern
Clear adhesive-backed vinyl
Masking tape
Mosaic pieces for project
Newspaper
Dish soap and water
Petroleum jelly
¾ in exterior grade plywood board
Galvanized hardware cloth (wire mesh)
Ready-mixed mortar cement
Portland cement
Latex polymer additive (optional)
Water
Tint (optional)
Sand

Tools

Apron
Safety glasses
Utility knife or scissors
Form/mold
Permanent waterproof fine-tipped marker and/or
    china marker
Cork-backed straightedge
Glass cutter
Tile and/or glass mosaic nippers
Running pliers
Breaking/grozing pliers
Smoothing device—carborundum stone, wet/dry
    sandpaper, diamond pad, or glass grinder
Small containers or jars
Sponge
Soft lint-free cloth
Tweezers and/or dental tools
Wire cutters
Rubber or latex gloves
Respirator or dust mask
Watertight mixing container
Trowel or wooden straightedge
Plastic sheet
Spray bottle
Screwdriver
Razor blades and/or paint scraper
Soft bristled brushes and/or toothbrush
Small garden spade or shovel

Choosing a form/mold

The garden stone and patio projects are made using a variation of the Indirect (Reverse) Method (p23) of mosaic construction. Individual pieces of tesserae are positioned on a sheet of clear adhesive-backed vinyl and placed in the bottom of a form or mold. A fine cement mixture is poured into the form/mold and allowed to cure for several days. The hardened concrete becomes the base/support structure that holds the many pieces of mosaic in place. Purchase round, square, rectangular, and hexagonal molds or use household or found objects to create novelty shapes and designs. For instructions on making a customized form, *see* Making Garden Stone Forms (p109).
NOTE   The bottom of the form/mold should be flat and have perpendicular sides. If sides are angled towards the center of the form/mold, the garden stone cannot be removed without damaging
the form/mold.

Choosing tesserae material

It is important to choose the correct tesserae material to fabricate a successful mosaic garden stone.
1   The face (surface) of tesserae should be smooth and flat. Use art glass, vitreous glass tesserae, or ceramic tile.
2   If you use tesserae created from textured glass or ceramic dinnerware, position pieces so the smoothest side will be on the top side of the garden stone. Uneven surfaces create spaces that cement can seep into which may lift tesserae from the vinyl and engulf them in cement.
3   Choose colorful and contrasting opaque materials for their reflective qualities but keep translucent glasses to a minimum (they often appear dull and discolored when surrounded by concrete). Iridescent glasses add shimmer and highlights.

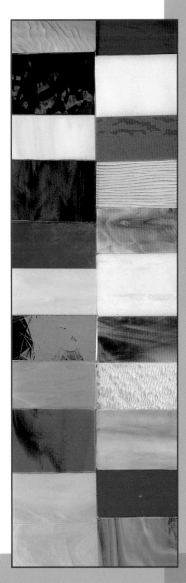

Preparing the pattern

1 Make 3 copies (p10) of pattern. Adjust pattern copies if any alterations have been made to the original. There must be a minimum space or line thickness of ⅛ in to ¼ in between each mosaic piece.

2 Use one pattern copy as a guide for cutting, breaking, and shaping mosaic pieces to correct size and shape. Use second copy to cut out any pattern piece requiring a template remembering to cut *inside* the pattern lines. Use third copy to place beneath clear adhesive-backed vinyl to act as a guide when laying tesserae.

3 Verify that the pattern fits within the form. Trim excess paper away from the outline of the third copy and place it flat and uncreased on the bottom of the form. Garden stones have been devised to have ¼ in to ½ in space between the tesserae along the perimeter of the pattern and the interior walls of the form. If you make pattern adjustments, be sure to adjust the other two copies as well.

4 Remove pattern from form. Place on a light table face down and trace the design lines onto the reverse side (or if using a window as a light source, the design should face away from you).

5 Tape pattern copy to a flat work surface, with reverse side facing up.

6 Cut a piece of clear, adhesive-backed vinyl, ½ in larger than the outside edges of the pattern. Peel the paper backing from the vinyl. Position the vinyl over the pattern taped to work surface, with the adhesive side facing up (do not stick it to the pattern). The pattern should be completely covered by the vinyl yet visible through it. Tape in place. Do not position tape within the pattern outline.

NOTE Use clear 8mm sandblast resist because of the strength of its adhesive and the thickness of the vinyl. Resist is available through most stained glass shops. Alternatively, use clear contact paper but its adhesive is not as strong.

Preparing mosaic pieces

1 Store same size, shape, and color tesserae pieces in small jars or containers until ready for use.

2 Using marker and pattern copies as a guide, trace (p10) distinctive configurations onto the material to be cut.

3 Cut (p11) each piece as required, *inside* the marker line.

4 Smooth and shape jagged edges (p19) to fit pattern. Pieces should fit within pattern lines with space of ⅛ in to ¼ in for the mortar cement to get around each tessera.

5 Clean each piece thoroughly with soap and water. Rinse with clean water.

6 Apply ceramic tile sealant to unglazed and porous

tesserae surfaces to prevent staining and water retention.

Placing mosaic pieces onto the vinyl

Turn each tessera over and place face down onto the vinyl in the correct position. Press the pieces firmly onto the resist. NOTE The pattern copy under the vinyl is the reverse of the pattern used to cut the pieces.

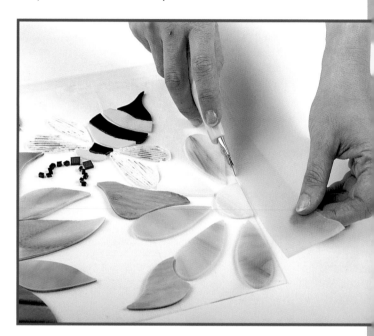

Trim away excess vinyl, as close to pattern edge as possible, without dislodging the glass pieces.

Preparing the form/mold

Coat sides, edges and corners, and a 1 in border around perimeter of bottom of the form/mold with a thin layer of petroleum jelly for effortless release of garden stone. NOTE Do not apply petroleum jelly to entire bottom of form/mold because it will act as a suction cup and prevent release of the garden stone.

Transferring mosaic pieces to the form/mold

1 Using a utility knife, cut away excess vinyl from perimeter of pattern, as close to edges of tesserae as possible without dislodging any pieces.

2 Carefully lift tesserae-laden vinyl and position in center of form/mold with mosaic pieces facing up. The vinyl prevents tesserae from moving while pouring the cement and acts as a barrier between form/mold and tesserae for easy removal from the form.

3 If form/mold is flexible in any way, such as plastic or resin, place a piece of plywood underneath for support. Plywood or metal forms will not require extra support.

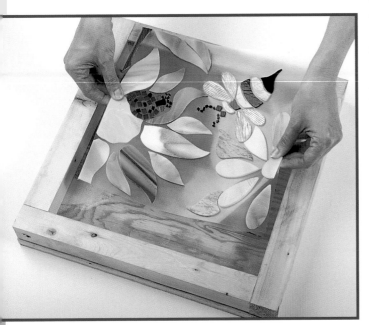

Carefully transfer the glass-laden vinyl and place it, face up in the center of the form/mold bottom.

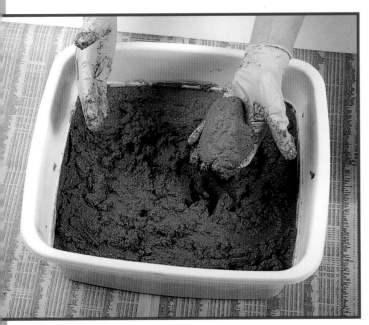

Mix cement thoroughly then squeeze a handful. If it holds its shape it is the correct consistency.

Reinforcement

Cut galvanized hardware cloth (wire mesh) to fit within the form/mold, making it approximately 1 in smaller on each side to prevent the wire from poking through the concrete on the sides of the garden stone.

Pouring the cement

Select a fine grade of ready-mixed cement or mortar mix to make a smooth finish on the surface of the garden stone. Add portland cement and/or a liquid latex polymer additive to the dry cement mixture for additional strength, flexibility, and water resistance. A more refined mortar mix will allow the cement to get between each tessera for a level surface and strong garden stone. Mixes with coarser grades of sand may leave a pitted surface. Follow the manufacturer's instructions.

NOTE   Avoid contact of cement mixtures (dry or wet) on skin areas, eyes, and clothing. Always wear safety glasses or goggles, work apron, rubber or latex gloves, and a respirator or dust mask when mixing and pouring cement (outdoors, if possible). Eye, skin areas, or clothing that come in contact with wet cement mixtures should be rinsed with water immediately.

1   Mix dry contents of entire mortar mix bag (average 55 lb or 25 kg) to evenly distribute bonding agents even if only a portion of the mix is needed. Mix in 4 to 5 cups of portland cement to ensure that enough of the agent is present.

NOTE Set aside 1 cup of dry mixture for use later if stone requires grouting.

2   Once dry ingredients have been mixed thoroughly, empty contents of bag (or amount needed) into a watertight container. Add water required (approx. 4 liters for full bag) and mix until well blended (moist but not runny or crumbly—a handful of cement when squeezed should maintain its shape when you open your fist). Allow cement to stand for 5 to 10 minutes, then re-mix thoroughly.

NOTE For additional strength and water resistance, liquid latex polymer additive can be used instead of, or in combination with, the required amount of water.

3   Carefully place a handful of the cement mixture into the form/mold. Gently smooth cement around edges and over tesserae, taking care not to dislodge any pieces from the vinyl. Gently pat the mixture to help the cement work its way into the spaces between the mosaic pieces and to release trapped air bubbles. Add enough cement to fill the form/mold halfway and continue patting for approximately

5 minutes. Softly tapping, with a hammer or mallet, on the work surface will also produce the same results.

4   Place the pre-cut reinforcement wire onto the cement and pour enough of the cement mixture on top to fill the form/mold. Again, gently pat for several minutes to release air bubbles. Entire depth of the garden stone should be 1½ in to 2 in, depending on the type and size of the form/mold used.

5   A thin layer of water on the surface of the stone is normal. Level the top with a trowel or a straight piece of wood.

Making your own cement mixture

Add 3 parts of fine grade sand to 1 part of portland cement. Mix dry ingredients thoroughly. Add water and mix until the desired consistency is achieved (p103). For additional strength and water resistance, a liquid latex polymer additive can be used instead of, or in combination with, the required amount of water.

Adding tints to the cement mixture

A wide array of tints are available that can be added to color your garden stone. The tints come in powder and liquid forms. Follow the manufacturer's instructions.

Curing

1   Set the poured garden stone form/mold on a level surface covered with plastic sheeting or newspaper. The form/mold should be kept out of direct sunlight and covered with plastic sheeting to prevent cement mixture from drying too quickly. Leave undisturbed for a minimum of 3 to 5 days in a location where temperatures will not drop to below freezing.

2   Once the cement has set, mist with water once a day to make sure it is not drying too quickly while curing.

Releasing the garden stone from the form/mold

1   Cover work surface with newspaper, turn the form over and lay face down.

2   To remove stone from a wood form (p105) unscrew the bottom piece from the attached side pieces. Unscrew two side pieces on opposing ends of the form so they can be pulled apart. Pull the two halves away from the garden stone, releasing it completely from the form. To reuse the form, simply screw the side and bottom pieces back together.

To remove stone from molds that cannot be taken apart (such as molded plastic), invert the mold and lay it face down onto the work surface. With one hand, tap on the bottom of the mold while slightly raising one side of the

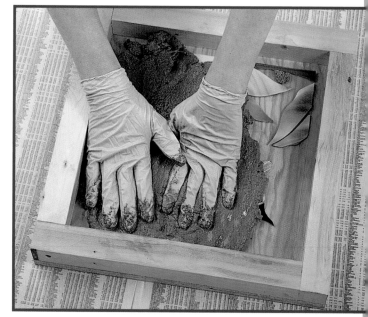

Gently pat the cement to help it work its way into the spaces between the mosaic pieces and to release air bubbles.

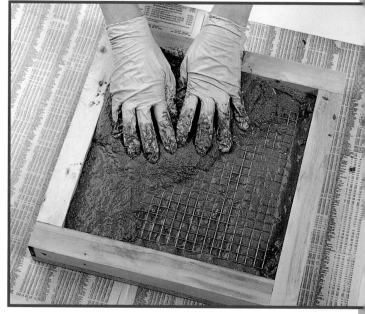

Fill the bottom half of the form with cement before adding the pre-cut reinforcement wire. Proceed to fill the form, covering the mesh.

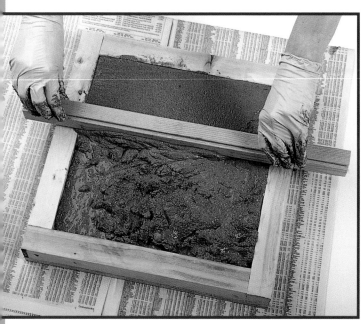

Level off the cement using a trowel or a straight piece of wood.

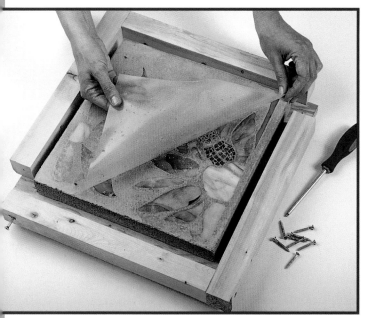

Unscrew the side pieces from the form base to remove the cured garden stone. Peel back the vinyl to reveal the stone surface.

mold off the table with the other hand. Rotate the mold while continuing to tap until the stone has released from the mold. Do not use too much force.

3   Peel clear adhesive-backed vinyl from top of garden stone. With a water-dampened sponge or cloth, wipe away thin film of cement on stone surface.

4   Excess cement can be removed with a soft bristled brush or by carefully scraping it away with a razor blade, paint scraper, or utility knife. Dental picks and toothbrushes can be used to clear away bits of cement caught in any grooves in the tesserae.

5   Small pits or gaps between tesserae can be filled in. Mix a small batch of ready-mix mortar (the cup that was set aside earlier) and smooth over the surface with a damp sponge or cloth. Remember to add tint if it was used in the original pour. Allow the mortar to dry to a thin haze for approximately 10 minutes and then wipe away excess with the damp sponge.

6   If you continue to have problems removing unwanted cement from the surface of the tesserae, try using muriatic acid (found at local hardware stores). Because of its hazardous properties, handle it with care, read the label carefully, and follow all safety precautions.

7   With a dry lint-free cloth, buff surface of finished mosaic garden stone.

8   It will take a minimum of 30 days for concrete to fully cure so handle garden stone with care. Do not allow to freeze. Do not walk on garden stones until fully cured.

Optional   Water-repellent concrete sealer can be applied to garden stone surface once it has fully cured to help prevent damage and cracking caused by moisture and freezing temperatures.

Installing finished mosaic garden stones

Finished mosaic garden stones can be nestled among flowers and foliage and moved about as the garden grows or changes. Or permanently set them into the ground.

1   Place the stone at the chosen site. With a small garden spade break the ground around the perimeter of the stone. Remove the stone and dig a hole the depth of the stone plus ½ in.

2   Fill the bottom of the hole with ½ in of sand (for drainage) and tamp it down, making sure it is level.

3   Place the garden stone in the hole making sure it is at ground level to prevent tripping or lawnmower damage.

Care and maintenance

Mosaic garden stones require little maintenance. Most stones can be left in the garden all year round regardless of changing weather conditions.

General care tips

1 Garden stones that are part of a water garden or exposed to a lot of moisture may require storage in a dry place during periods of freezing and thawing.

2 Stains and mildew, can be removed by scrubbing the surface with a diluted solution of chlorine bleach and water.

3 If a sealant has been applied to the surface it may wear off over time. Reapply sealant according to manufacturer's instructions.

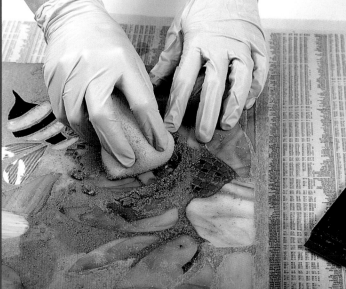

Small pits or gaps between the pieces can be filled by applying a small amount of mortar mix.

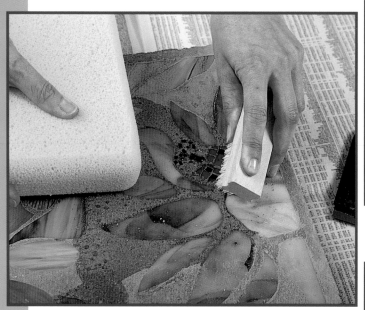

Remove the thin layer of cement from the garden stone surface with a damp sponge and a soft bristled brush.

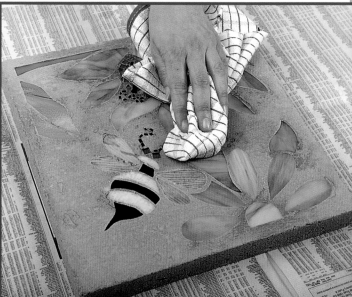

Buff the finished garden stone surface with a soft lint-free cloth.

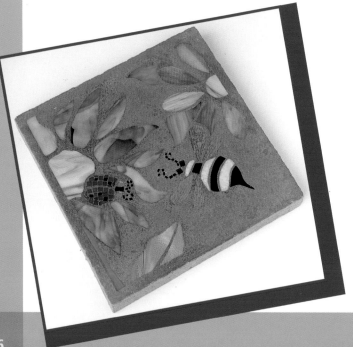

Common problems and solutions

Read instructions before beginning a project and follow the procedure in the correct sequence for best results.

Surface of the garden stone is pitted

To prevent

• A space (interstice) at least ⅛ in to ¼ in wide must be present between each tesserae to allow cement mixture to surround each piece and fill the air spaces.

• Use a fine grade of ready-made mortar mix or a fine grade of sand if you make your own cement. Cement mixtures with coarse sand particles may not fit between glass pieces.

• After filling the mold with the wet cement mixture, release trapped air bubbles and pockets by gently patting the cement or lightly tapping the worktable surface with a mallet or hammer.

To correct

• Fill in pits and level the surface of the garden stone by re-grouting.

Tesserae are immersed in the cement

To prevent

• Tesserae must be cleaned thoroughly before placing on the clear adhesive-backed vinyl. Avoid getting petroleum jelly on the tesserae or the vinyl.

• Firmly press the smoothest side of the tesserae onto the sticky side of the vinyl so wet cement mixture won't seep between the tesserae and the vinyl.

• For strong adhesion, use 8mm clear sandblast resist. Vinyl contact paper (sometimes referred to as shelf paper) with a strong tack can also be used. To maintain adhesive integrity, do not place anything else on vinyl.

• When releasing air bubbles (above) do not tap too hard or tesserae may dislodge from vinyl.

To correct

• When a tessera is partially covered by cement, scrape away excess with a razor blade, paint scraper, or utility knife. Dental picks can be used to dig cement out of surface grooves.

• If a tessera is completely immersed check the garden stone surface for an outline of the piece and scrape away the cement with a razor blade. Mix and apply a small amount of cement to smooth surface over gouges or unevenness caused by excavating the tessera.

• If you are not sure where the tessera is buried, leave it undisturbed. Once the stone has been situated in the garden or walkway, the concealed piece will probably not be missed.

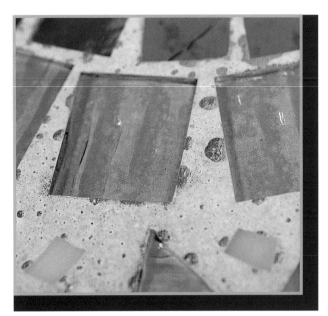

Pitted surfaces can be filled by regrouting with mortar mix.

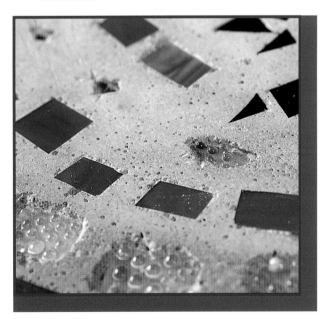

When tesserae are immersed in cement scrape away excess, lift out tessera, and re-cement in place.

Tesserae are falling off the garden stone surface

To prevent

• Spaces between tesserae should be at least ⅛ in. Large tesserae pieces tend to lift off the surface whereas smaller ones are easily held in place by the cement.

• Cement ingredients must be thoroughly mixed. Adding portland cement to the dry components will ensure that enough of this bonding agent is present in the mix. Use a liquid latex polymer additive for some or all of the water. Store unused dry ingredients indoors in a moisture-free environment.

• When transferring the sheet of tesserae-laden clear adhesive-backed vinyl into the form/mold, position the vinyl with a minimum ¼ in space between edges of form/mold and the mosaic pieces so they are completely surrounded by the concrete. Pieces that are too close to outside edge may become detached or easily pried away.

• Do not move a poured garden stone until the cement has cured and become concrete. Place flexible plastic molds on a sturdy plywood sheet to transport so tesserae don't move.

To correct

• Tesserae that have come away from the garden stone surface can be reattached. Use a utility knife to smooth out inside edges and bottom of the hole and remove debris. Spread a layer of water-resistant tile adhesive on side edges and bottom of the tessera and press into the hole. Allow to dry for a minimum of 24 hours. Grout around the piece and the opening with a small amount of wet cement mixture. Buff with a dry cloth once the cement has set completely.

Edges of garden stone are crumbling and breaking away

To prevent

• Make sure cement ingredients are well mixed. Add additional portland cement and/or a latex polymer additive for supplementary bonding strength. Follow the manufacturer's instructions carefully.

• Concrete must have at least 3 to 5 days to cure and harden before removing from the mold. While curing, cover the form/mold with a plastic sheet and mist with water once a day to prevent the cement from drying too quickly. Keep out of direct sunlight.

To correct

• Strengthen the garden stone and improve the appearance by re-grouting. Mix a portion of the wet cement mixture and apply to damaged areas. With your hands (wear protective gloves) or a trowel, smooth cement onto the stone and shape it to the correct dimensions. Cover with a plastic sheet and let dry slowly, misting occasionally. Once hardened,

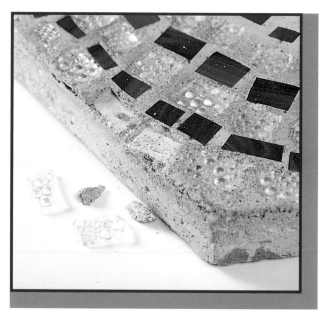

Mosaic pieces can become dislodged if they are positioned too close to the garden stone edge or if the cement is mixed improperly.

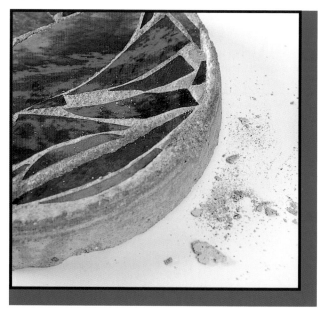

Always read and follow the cement manufacturer's directions carefully. Crumbling edges can be regrouted.

clean excess concrete off the surface of any affected mosaic pieces.

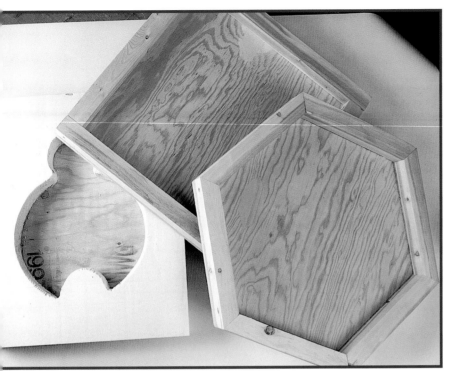

NOTE Use ¾ in exterior grade plywood. A garden stone should be approximately 1½ in to 2 in deep, so 2 in x 2 in framing lumber can be used to make the sides of the form. The sides provide support and contain the wet cement mixture within the form until it sets and becomes concrete.

To make the base of the form

1 Measure the width and the height of the garden stone pattern. Add 3 in to each measurement to allow room for the attachment of side pieces. For example, a 12 in x 12 in square garden stone requires a plywood base piece measuring 15 in x 15 in.

2 With a marking pen and straightedge, mark the dimensions required for the base piece onto the plywood sheet.

3 Cut out, using a wood saw.

To make the side pieces for the form

4 Measure each side of the pattern outline. For each side piece, add 1½ in to the measurement, mark and cut the 2 in x 2 in framing lumber. For a square garden stone pattern measuring 12 in along each side, cut four lengths that each measure 13½ in.

Aligning and attaching the side pieces to the base of the form

5 Using the pattern as a guide, lay a side piece along the corresponding edge of the garden stone outline. One end of the piece should start at a corner (where two sides meet at a right angle) with the other end extending past the pattern outline, approximately 1½ in.

6 Align the next side piece. Butt one end of the second piece against the overlap of the first side piece. As with the preceding side, the opposite end of the piece will extend past the pattern outline by approximately 1½ in. Fasten the two pieces together with a wood screw.

7 Repeat step 6 to align and fasten each of the two remaining side pieces, creating a four-sided frame. Verify that each of the four corners of the frame is square, using a carpenter's square.

8 Place the plywood base piece on top of this frame and fasten base to frame, using two wood screws per side.

9 Smooth any rough surfaces or edges on the wood form with sandpaper.

Making garden stone forms
Making a form/mold

Wood forms (square, rectangle, hexagon, octagon, etc.) are easy to make and can be used many times. All that is required are a few woodworking tools and the knowledge to use them safely. When using any power tool, read the manufacturer's directions and follow all safety guidelines and precautions. Always wear a work apron and safety glasses.

Materials
1 copy of pattern
¾ in exterior grade plywood
2 in x 2 in (actually 1½ in x 1½ in) framing lumber
#8 wood screws (2½ in long)
Sandpaper

Tools
Apron
Safety glasses
Marking pen or pencil
Carpenter's square
Straightedge
Wood saw
Power drill
Screwdriver

NOTE   To make wood screws easier to twist in, mark and pre-drill holes in side pieces and base. Using wood screws allows form to be taken apart if the finished garden stone cannot be easily removed.

Styrofoam and plywood forms

Irregular shaped and curving forms can be made with styrofoam and plywood. Use high density foam insulation like that used in the construction industry, available at local hardware stores. Forms can be used several times when handled with care.

Materials
1 copy of pattern
Carbon paper
Masking tape
Styrofoam sheet (approx. 1½ to 2 in thick)
¾ in exterior grade plywood
2 in drywall screws

Tools
Apron
Safety glasses
Marking pen or pencil
Utility knife
Wood saw
Power drill

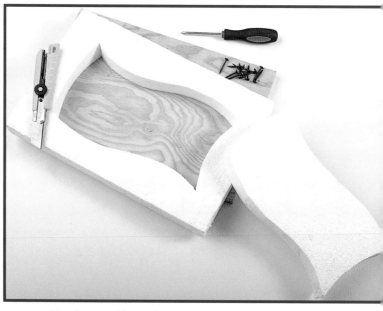

Styrofoam molds can be cut easily into irregular shapes for any project.

1   Place carbon paper face down, over the center of the styrofoam sheet. Position pattern copy over carbon paper and fasten in place with masking tape.
2   Trace the outline of the pattern onto the styrofoam sheet. The styrofoam must be large enough to allow at least 2 in between pattern outline and the edge of the sheet. Remove carbon and pattern copy.
3   For a clean edge, use a utility knife held *perpendicular* to styrofoam surface to cut along the traced outline. *Do not angle knife.*
4   Remove styrofoam piece from sheet.
5   Cut a plywood base piece the same size as the styrofoam sheet.
6   Place plywood base on top of the styrofoam sheet.
7   Use drywall screws to attach plywood to the styrofoam. Countersink screws so they are level with plywood surface.
NOTE   Apply a thin layer of petroleum jelly to sides and inside edges of all forms and molds, regardless of the materials used in their construction.

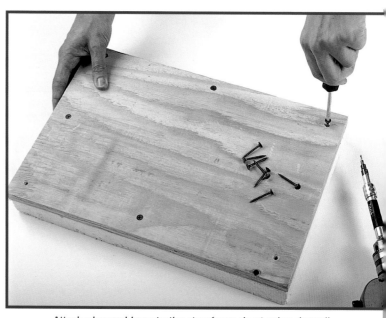

Attach plywood base to the styrofoam sheet using drywall screws. With care, styrofoam molds can be used many times.

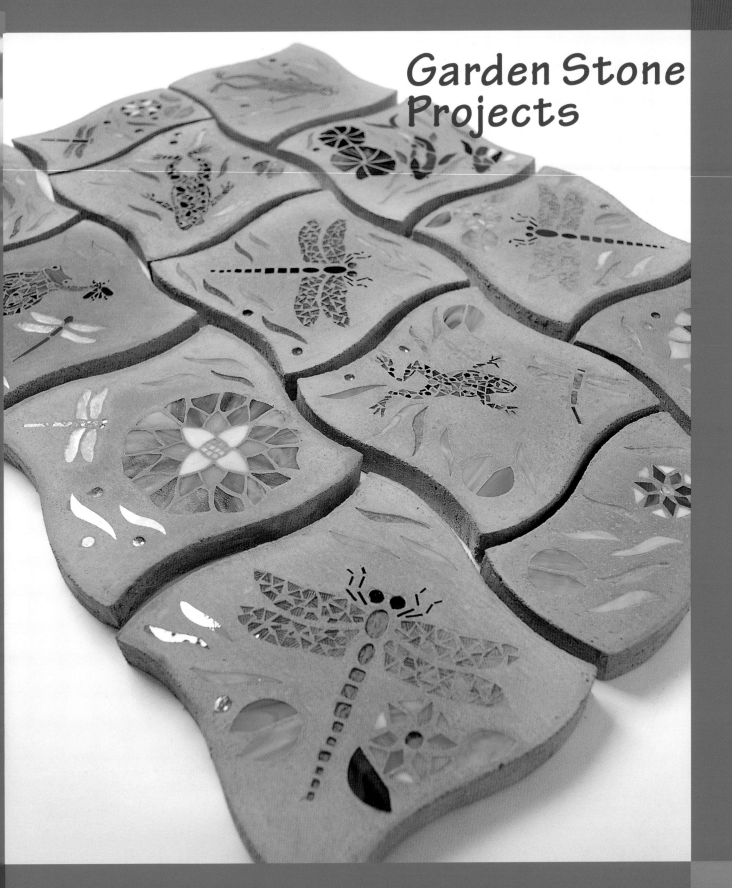

Garden Stone Projects

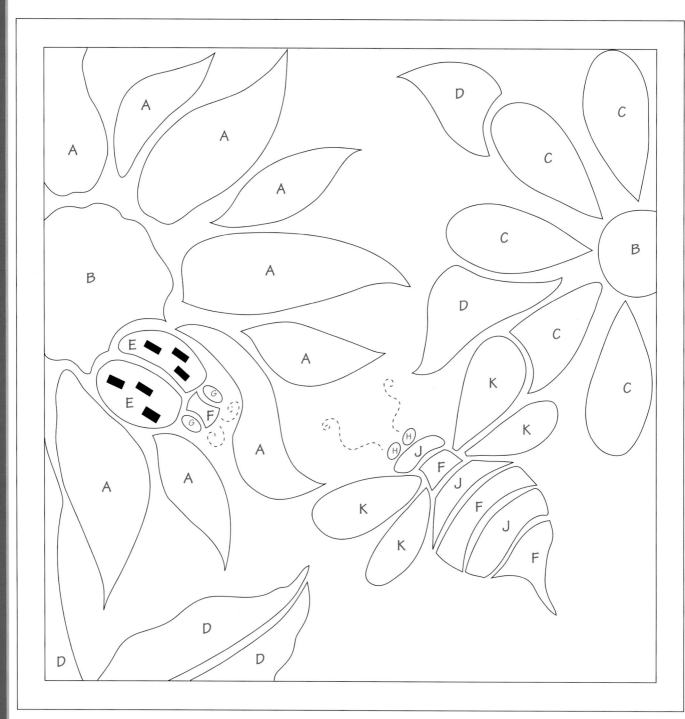

F ▬ ------ line indicates small black
tesserae used for antennae

Buzz Meets Lily

garden stone

Mold size   **12 in square**

Wet cement mixture required   **18 cups**

Mosaic material required

Letters refer to the type and quantity of art glass used on pattern pieces (p112).

The quantities and types of materials listed are the minimum requirements for completing this project as illustrated, but materials may be substituted, if desired.

A   6 in x 12 in opaque lavender and dark purple streaky
B   3 in x 4 in opaque yellow with pink and white streaky
C   3 in x 8 in translucent pink with opaque white streaky
D   6 in x 6 in opaque medium green with white streaky
E   2 in x 2 in opaque red
F   4 in x 4 in black
G   1 in x 1 in mirrored light amber semi-antique
H   1 in x 1 in mirrored dark blue semi-antique
J   3 in x 3 in opaque yellow ring mottle
K   3 in x 5 in iridescent clear textured
NOTE   The letter I is not used in this listing.

Instructions

This garden stone is constructed following instructions given for Mosaic Garden and Patio Stones—Basic Steps (p101).

Use a 12 in x 12 in square wood mold. To make your own garden stone form, refer to Wood Forms (p109) for specific instructions.

NOTE Though not always the best or most visible choice for a garden stone, iridescent clear textured glass (K) can achieve the gossamer effect that characterizes insect wings. Be sure to lay smooth side of glass wing pieces down onto the adhesive-backed vinyl. If the textured side of glass is adhered to the vinyl, the wet cement mixture may work its way into crevices in the glass surface causing pieces to lift from the vinyl and becoming immersed in concrete.

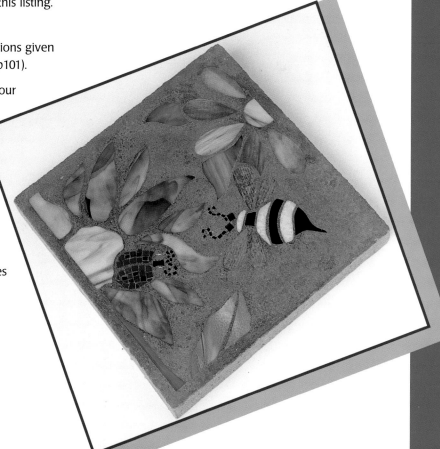

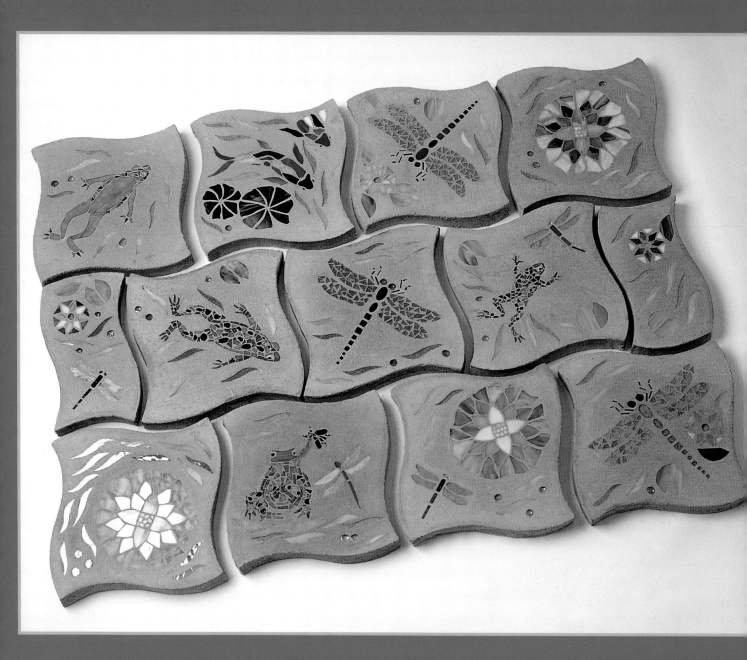

Water Garden

patio stones

Form/mold required   interlocking forms A, B, C

Wet cement mixture required   A 16 cups / B 16 cups / C 8 cups

Mosaic material required

 Assorted art glasses in green, orange, red, pink, yellow, blue, iridescent clear textured, and black

 Assortment of glass nuggets

Instructions

To create the Water Garden patio choose designs from frogs, water lilies, dragonflies, lily pads, and koi fish patterns illustrated on pp118-120. Mix and match stones to assemble the patio layout.

1   Make garden stone forms or adapt the patterns to fit a form/mold already acquired. Determine the number of garden stones necessary to complete the patio.

• Layout #1 is an undulating grid-like pattern comprised of garden stones made using pattern form A (p116).

• Layout #2 uses pattern forms A, B, and C to make alternating rows of garden stones in a staggered wave pattern (p117). Rows comprised solely of poured garden stones using pattern form A are then alternated with staggered rows of garden stones made in form B (the *reverse* shape of pattern form A). A garden stone fabricated in form C is then placed at either end of this second set of stones to align and even out the rows. Refer to Styrofoam and Plywood Forms (p110) for specific instructions for making forms for this project.

2   Construct each garden stone by following the instructions given for Mosaic Garden and Patio Stones—Basic Steps (p101).

NOTE

• Unify the overall theme of the patio by placing several ripple-shaped tesserae in each garden stone. Tesserae made from iridescent clear textured glass and an iridescent soft blue glass create a shimmering effect. Be sure to lay the smooth iridescent side of the pieces down onto the adhesive-backed vinyl. If the textured side of the glass is adhered to the vinyl, the wet cement mixture may work its way into crevices in the glass causing the pieces to lift from the vinyl and becoming immersed in the concrete.

• When assembling a large patio, make a number of forms so that the concrete for several garden stones can be mixed and poured at one time.

• Glass nuggets make interesting accents when used as dragonfly eyes, bubbles of water, and centers for water lilies. Be sure to press the flat bottom side of a glass nugget onto the adhesive-backed vinyl. Placing the rounded side of a nugget face down may result in its detachment from the vinyl. Cut glass pieces can be substituted for the glass nuggets.

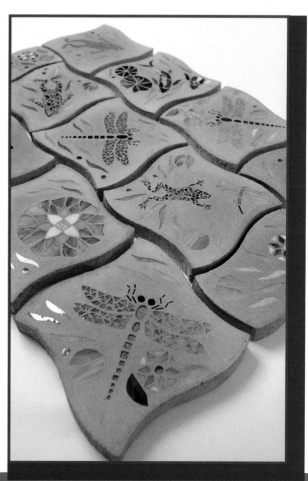

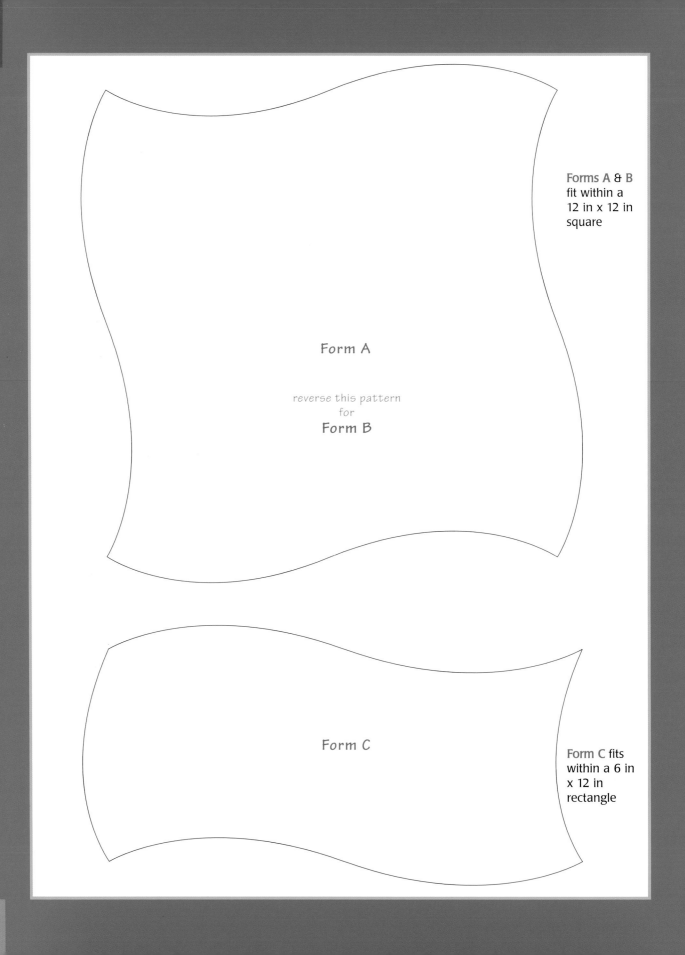

Forms A & B
fit within a
12 in x 12 in
square

Form A

reverse this pattern
for
Form B

Form C

Form C fits
within a 6 in
x 12 in
rectangle

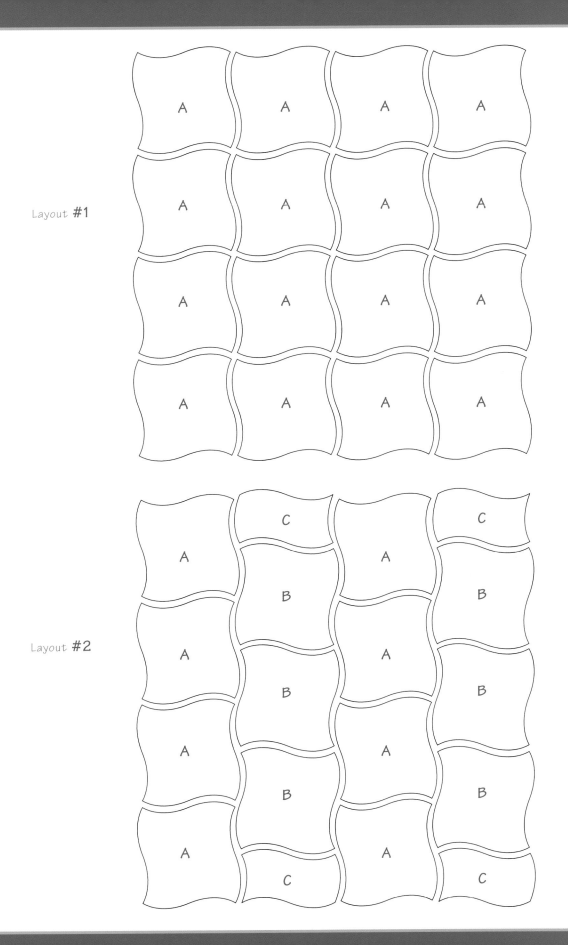

Layout #1

Layout #2

117

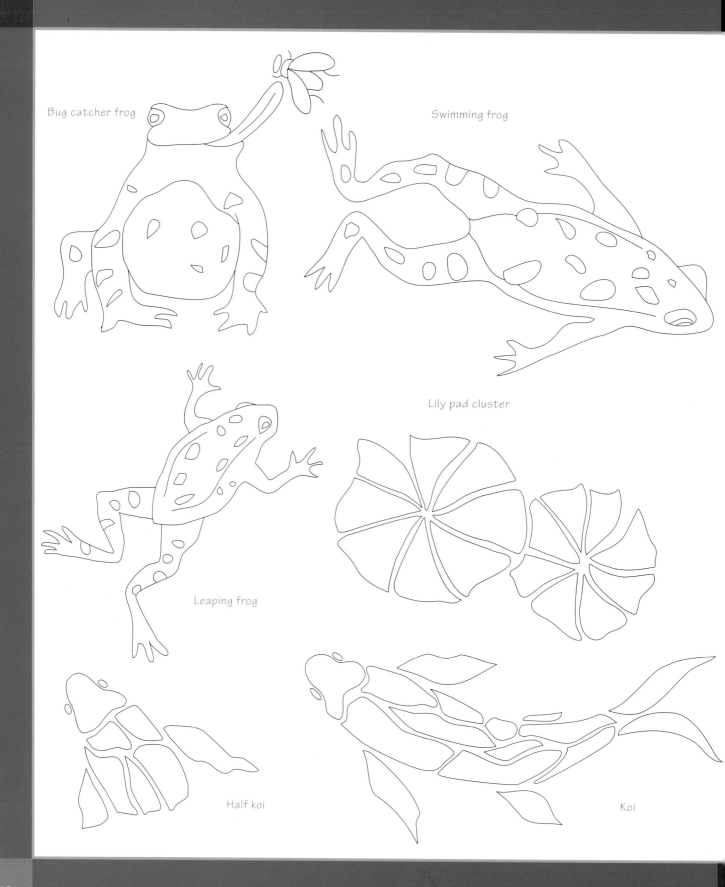

Bug catcher frog

Swimming frog

Lily pad cluster

Leaping frog

Half koi

Koi

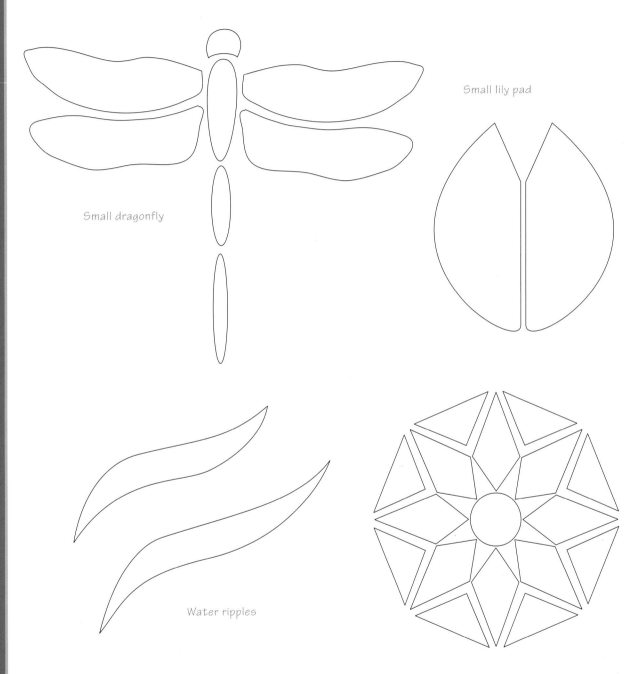

Small lily pad

Small dragonfly

Water ripples

Small waterlily

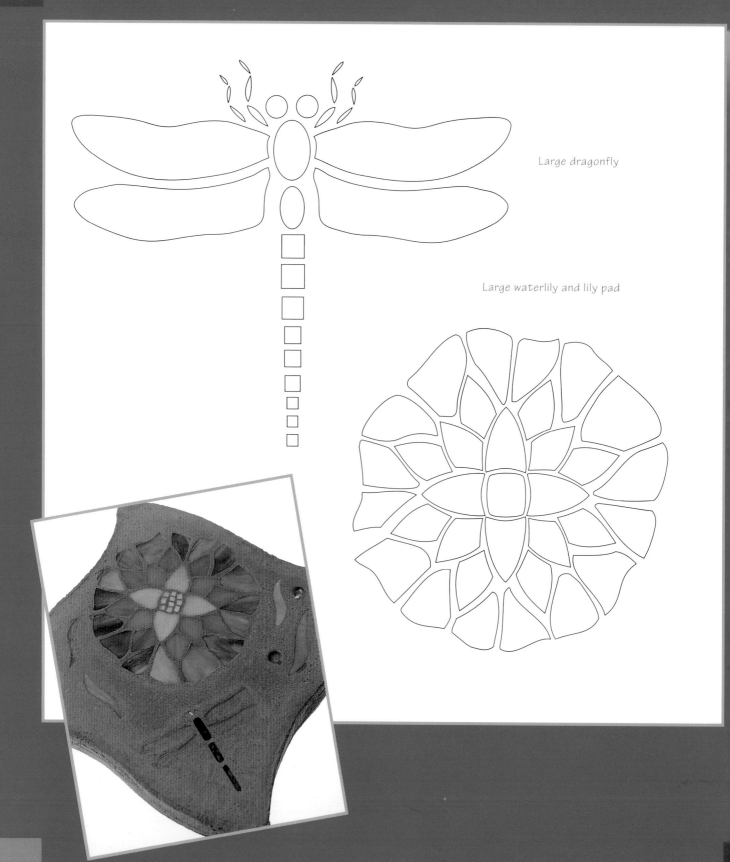

Large dragonfly

Large waterlily and lily pad

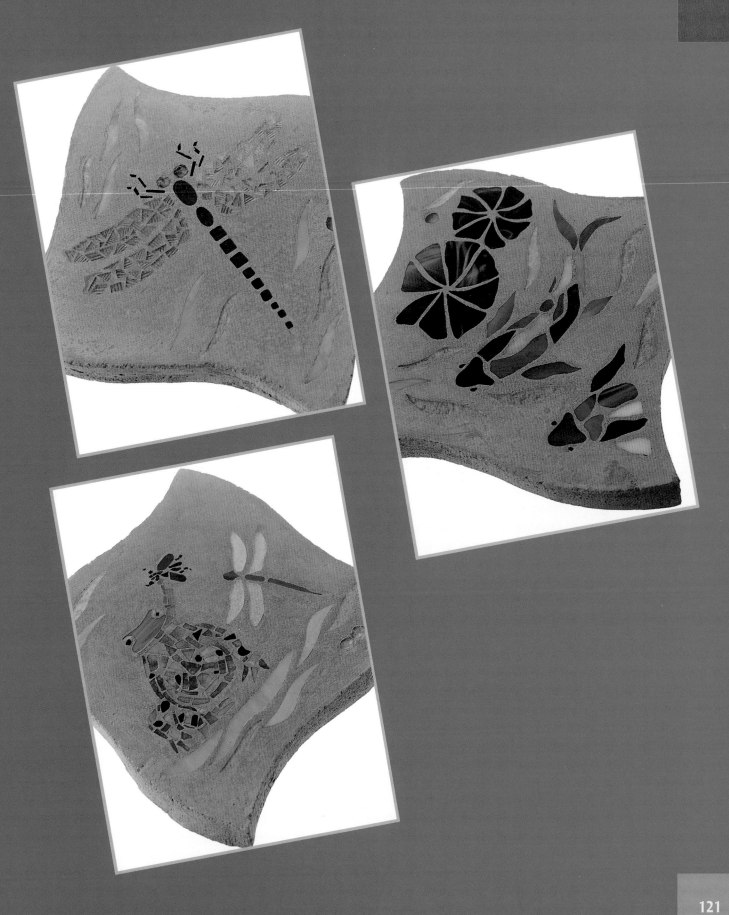

Mosaic Ideas for the Garden

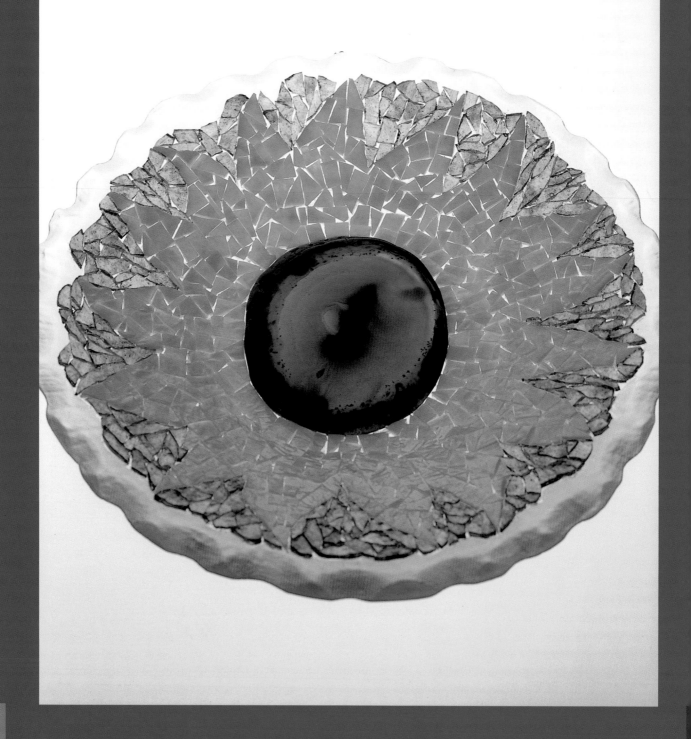

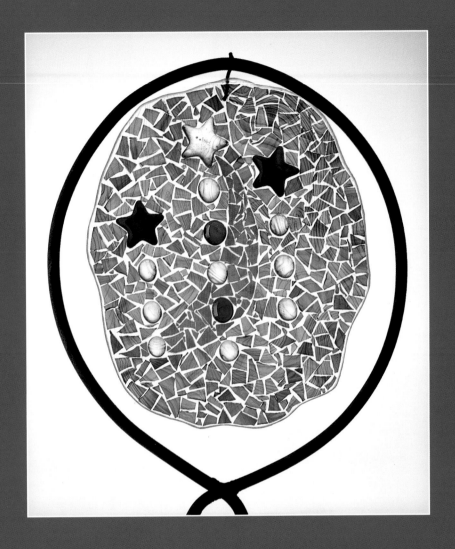

Moonlight, Starlight
Translucent glass hangings can be used in the garden when hung from a metal stand. Glass stars and nuggets become three-dimensional shooting stars enveloped by a night sky and a crescent moon made from art glass tesserae.
Hanging is not grouted, to maintain soft, dreamy quality.

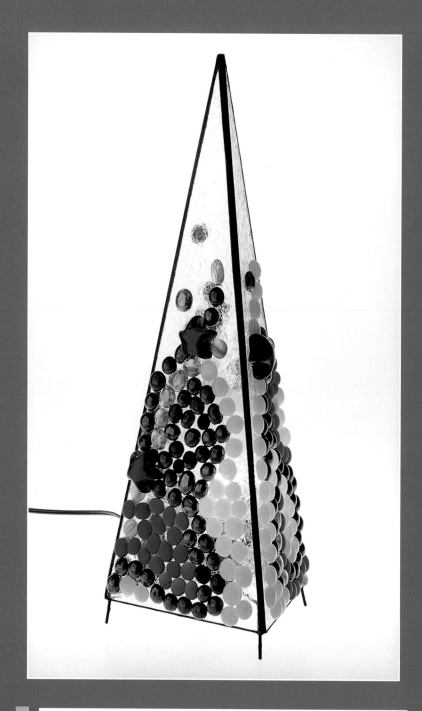

Starlight

The support structure for this garden light is fabricated by soldering together panels of clear textured art glass and then inserting an electrical fixture inside. To maintain clarity and water resistance use clear silicone to adhere glass nuggets and stars directly to the support structure. No grout is used to fill the spaces between each piece.

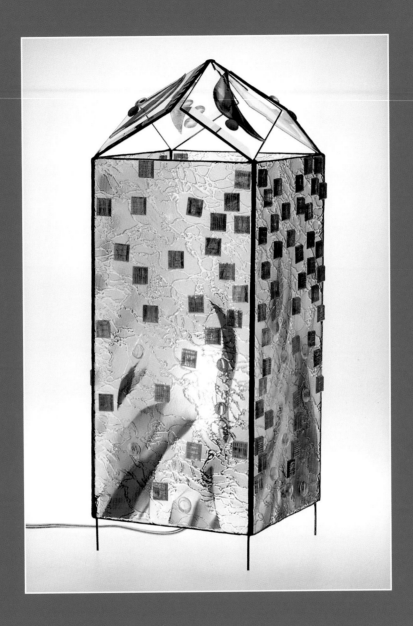

Garden Tower

This ultra-modern garden sculpture is constructed from clear textured art glass and beveled glass pieces. Exterior is decorated with translucent glass mosaic tiles containing wisps of copper and glass nuggets. Shaped colored glass tesserae are adhered to the interior. Piece is illuminated by an electrical fixture placed inside. This sculpture is an example of the new ways mosaic materials can be used and combined with other mediums.

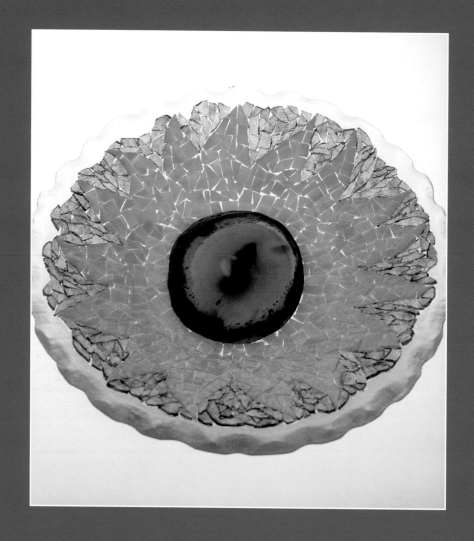

Sunflower

The large geode that is the center of the sunflower is surrounded by petals and background foliage formed from random-shaped (p22) art glass tesserae. All mosaic pieces are adhered to the clear decorative platter with non-toxic clear silicone. Piece is not grouted. This translucent mosaic can be used as decorative bird bath or garden water dish.

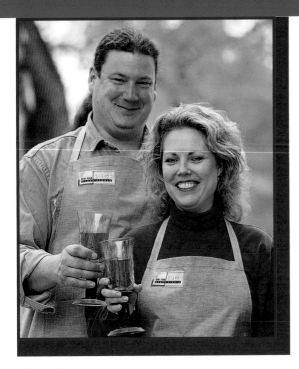

About the authors

George W. Shannon and Pat Torlen own and operate On the Edge Glass Studio in Winnipeg, Canada. They teach as well as design and fabricate commissioned works for commercial and residential clientele utilizing traditional and contemporary stained glass techniques, sandblasting, kiln work, and mosaic construction. In 1999, they were commissioned to create a sandcarved and airbrushed glass wall for the Air Canada Maple Leaf Lounge at the Winnipeg International Airport. They received a 1999-2000 Modern Liturgy Visuals Arts Award for the Trinity Series of communion chalices and vessels they created for the Parish of St. Timothy (shown above).

Through the years, both artists have participated in intensive workshops and classes given by internationally renowned glass artists such as Irene Frolic, Marc Gibeau, Mitchell Gaudet, Paul Marioni, Virginia Gabaldo, Richard Millard, Rachel Mesrahi, Tim O'Neill, and Dan Fenton. George has attended Pilchuck Glass School in Stanwood, Washington, and Pat was a coordinator and participant in a glass casting course taught at the University of Manitoba. This book is the result of their quest to bring new ideas and approaches to their work with mosaics. George and Pat are the authors of three other books published by Sterling/Tamos: *Stained Glass: Projects & Patterns*; *Stained Glass Mosaics: Projects & Patterns*; and *Decorative Glass: Sandblasting, Copper Foil & Leaded Stained Glass Projects & Patterns*.

Index